THE FALLACY OF STAR WARS

D0960331

THE FALLACY OF STAR WARS

**BASED ON STUDIES
CONDUCTED BY THE
UNION OF CONCERNED SCIENTISTS**

*and co-chaired by Richard L. Garwin,
Kurt Gottfried, and Henry W. Kendall*

Edited by John Tirman

**VINTAGE BOOKS
A DIVISION OF RANDOM HOUSE
NEW YORK**

A VINTAGE ORIGINAL, October 1984
FIRST EDITION

A portion of this work was printed in *The New York
Review of Books*.

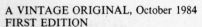

Library of Congress Cataloging in Publication Data
Main entry under title:
The fallacy of star wars.
    Bibliography: p.
    1. Space weapons. 2. Anti-satellite weapons.
3. Ballistic missile defenses. 4. United States—
Military policy. 5. Soviet Union—Military policy.
I. Union of Concerned Scientists.
UG1530.S63 1984   355.8′25   84-13129
ISBN 0-394-72894-7

Cover art and text illustrations by Jon Lomberg

Designed by Naomi Osnos

Manufactured in the United States of America
9 8 7 6 5 4 3 2
First Edition

Science and politics are often at loggerheads in America. The conflict between the two has rarely been more stark than in the current debate over "Star Wars"—not the fantasy of film director George Lucas, but the political fantasy of Ronald Reagan. Since Mr. Reagan's inauguration in 1981, the issues of war and peace have become more prominent than at any time since America's military involvement in Indochina. And few aspects of the national awakening to the threat of nuclear war have provoked a more spirited reaction than the president's determination to build space weapons.

The debate over "Star Wars"—ballistic missile defense—and the Air Force program to build anti-satellite (ASAT) weapons is plagued by competing sets of beliefs and controversies over facts. Claims and counterclaims about technical feasibility, Soviet intentions, and treaty violations swirl around like a maelstrom. The Reagan administration openly acknowledges that its vision of space-based missile defense—the hope to destroy Russian nuclear missiles during war before they reach the United States—is predicated on major scientific and technological breakthroughs in several different fields. The quite attainable technology of ASATs is debated on the equally esoteric grounds of strategic doctrine and speculations about Soviet behavior. Small wonder that the entire subject of space weapons is a source of confusion and misperceptions by the public and policymakers.

In February 1983, the Union of Concerned Scientists (UCS) set out to study the ASAT issue. Soon after, President Reagan announced his wish to build a ballistic missile defense (BMD), an announcement that changed the entire landscape of the space weapons debate. In the autumn of 1983, UCS began to explore the technical and policy contours of BMD as well. This book combines those two studies with a new introduction that explains the evolution of strategic doctrine and the recurring issue of missile defense.

To an important extent, the UCS activities on space weapons have been motivated by the alarming gap in public understanding of these policy initiatives. When we began our work in early 1983, the level of knowledge and analysis in Congress, the news media, and the public at large was dismally low. Such a state of affairs is not surprising; one can hardly expect the average citizen, reporter, or member of Congress to be steeped in the technicalities of laser weapons, homing vehicles, and the like. If the course of the debate on Capitol Hill is any indication, however, the efforts to raise awareness about anti-satellite weapons and missile defense have been rather successful, a signal that science and politics can coexist productively.

Seldom has an arms issue moved as quickly from the periphery to the center of the policy arena as the space weapons issue. Still an obscure subject as the 1980s began, space weapons suddenly emerged during 1983 and 1984 as a focus of attention and controversy in Congress, among the public at large, and internationally. As in the case of the anti-ballistic missile (ABM) debate fifteen years earlier, this shift came about through a combination of new government policies and a vigorous challenge to those policies by the scientific community.

The current debate can be traced to the mid 1970s, when the Soviets resumed testing an ASAT developed several years earlier. The Carter administration responded to this program with a two-track policy: negotiations toward a treaty that would restrict or possibly ban ASATs, and development of an ASAT interceptor to be launched from an F-15 jet.

Interest in the issue began to grow during the second year of the Reagan administration as the outlines of the president's military space policy emerged. In tone and substance, the new policy promised a more assertive stance, emphasizing stronger U.S. military capabilities in space and downplaying negotiations with the Soviets. Mr. Reagan announced in a July 4, 1982, address that the U.S. would proceed with development of the F-15 ASAT to deter Soviet attack on U.S. satellites and "to deny any adversary the use of space-based systems that provide support to hostile military forces." The creation of an Air Force Space Command the same year underscored the new emphasis on space as a military domain.

The administration declared that it would consider pursuing space arms control measures "should those measures be compatible with United States national security," but it showed no inclination to resume the suspended ASAT talks. The Soviets had offered a draft treaty banning space weapons at the United Nations the previous summer. Although the administration dismissed this initiative as unworthy of serious response, there was a growing sentiment in the scientific and arms control communities that negotiations must be explored before the United States became irrevocably committed to a space arms race.

A petition to ban space weapons, circulated by Richard Garwin and Carl Sagan in February 1983, was signed by a large number of eminent scientists, pioneers of the nation's civilian space program, and retired military officers, and sent to the president, Soviet Chairman Yuri Andropov, and other world leaders. The Union of Concerned Scientists drafted the report on ASATs and the proposed U.S.-Soviet treaty that are reproduced in this book, and presented them to the Senate Foreign Relations Committee in May 1983. In cooperation with the Federation of American Scientists and other expert groups, UCS played a key role in spreading interest and information on space weapons among members of Congress and their staffs.

This incipient movement became a force to be reckoned with in the aftermath of the president's March 1983 "Star Wars" speech, which immediately placed the space weapons issue in the spotlight. Over the remainder of the year, congressional activity on military space matters increased dramatically and for the first time attracted widespread press attention. Growing apprehension about the administration ASAT policy was expressed in several legislative initiatives aimed at a resumption of talks with the Soviets.

Meanwhile, space weapons enthusiasts in Congress pressed from the other direction, without notable success, for an acceleration of U.S. military space programs. Congressman Ken Kramer of Colorado introduced a "People Protection Act" designed to create a bureaucratic juggernaut on behalf of the Star Wars policy, and Senator Malcolm Wallop of Wyoming pushed for early deployment of laser weapons in a resolution that was soundly defeated.

In July 1983, the Senate unanimously adopted an amendment to the defense authorization bill to restrain the administration's ASAT testing plans. Proposed by Senator Paul Tsongas of Massachusetts, the amendment prohibits the testing of the F-15 system against a space object unless the president certifies that the United States is endeavoring in good faith to negotiate an ASAT treaty or, pending such an agreement, that testing is necessary to prevent clear and irrevocable harm to U.S. national security. The same month, the Senate Foreign Relations Committee adopted Resolution S.R. 129, calling on the president to implement a three-stage strategy leading to a space weapons ban: first, to seek a mutual, verifiable moratorium of limited duration on ASAT space flight tests; second, to immediately resume bilateral negotiations with the Soviets to ban the testing, production, deployment, and use of ASAT weapons; and third, to expand these negotiations to pursue a ban on all future space-based and space-directed weapons.

Pressure on the administration increased in August when nine U.S. senators met in Moscow with Chairman Andropov. Andropov used the meeting to announce a unilateral Soviet moratorium on ASAT test launches, subject to similar U.S. restraint, and to declare Soviet willingness to negotiate the elimination of existing ASATs and banning of new ones. The proposal was presented at the United Nations as a new draft treaty, one that many observers viewed as a great improvement on the 1981 Soviet draft. This development prompted the Senate Foreign Relations Committee to report that "most members conclude that the latest Soviet initiative would justify the early resumption of bilateral negotiations."

In the fall of 1983, Congress for the first time showed a willingness to use its budget leverage to pressure the administration on ASAT negotiations. The House of Representatives deleted $19 million in procurement funds from the ASAT budget and instructed the administration to produce a comprehensive report explaining its ASAT arms control policy. The full Congress restored the money, but ordered it withheld until forty-five days after the administration's report.

With the release of the White House report on March 31, 1984, the lines seemed drawn. The administration virtually ruled out ASAT negotiations and reiterated its commitment to space weapons on military grounds. This approach seemed unlikely to satisfy Congress and promised future confrontations over the ASAT and Star Wars budgets. Indeed, the House of Representatives voted decisively in May to withhold funding for future ASAT tests. The first round of hearings on the Strategic Defense Initiative in the spring of 1984 found administration officials themselves on the defensive in the face of an increasingly skeptical Congress. It appeared that Congress would demonstrate its disapproval in the best way it knows how—by cutting the administration's request for funding Star Wars and ASATs.

This book is divided into three parts. The first gives the historical background of the space weapons issue. The second is a revised version of the UCS report *Space-Based Missile Defense*, which was released in March 1984. The third part is an updated and expanded version of the May 1983 testimony and draft treaty on ASATs, which was published subsequently as a UCS report, *Anti-Satellite Weapons: Arms Control or Arms Race?*

Both reports are the product of distinguished panels of scientists and defense experts convened by UCS to analyze these separate, but related, questions. The two panels are listed following the preface. There is considerable overlap of the members of the panels, and for good reason: they are among the nation's leading authorities on these subjects, bringing many years of experience at the highest levels of government and academia to the study of the current administration's policy. The high standard of their contributions is reflected in the fact that both of the UCS studies on space weapons have become touchstones of the debate in Congress, the national security community, and the administration itself.

The reader will readily see that the tone and approach of the two reports are different. The BMD report, Part II of this book, is principally an assessment of the technologies envisaged for a missile defense. As such, several of the chapters are rather technical in nature. Every effort to make these discussions comprehensible to the nonscientist has been made. Because the issue *is* necessarily technical—that is, the debate hinges on the technical feasibility of these Star Wars weapons —it is essential to assess the proposed BMD systems with meticulous scientific detail. Readers who are not interested in that depth of analysis can skip over Chapters 5 and 6 and proceed to the summary in Chapter 7 and the political discussion of Chapter 8. At the other extreme, readers interested in the technical considerations should request the report, "Some Technical Aspects of Space-Based Ballistic Missile Defense," available from UCS in Cambridge, Massachusetts 02238. The ASAT report, Part III of this book, originated as Senate testimony to support the UCS draft treaty. As such, its scope is somewhat narrower, but it is less challenging technically. Of particular interest in Part III is an addition, Chapter 15, which evaluates the Reagan administration's March 1984 policy statement on ASATs. It should be added that because of the origin of these reports, there is a certain amount of redundancy from time to time, but we wished to preserve the reports largely as written.

The UCS activities on space weapons are due in large measure to Kurt Gottfried, professor of physics and nuclear studies at Cornell University, a director of UCS, and the principal author of this book; and to Henry W. Kendall, professor of physics at MIT and UCS chairman. Professor Gottfried chaired the ASAT panel and co-chaired, with Professor Kendall, the BMD study. The proposal that a private group formulate an ASAT test ban treaty that would satisfy U.S. interests is due to Richard L. Garwin, who has made invaluable contributions to all facets of the book. Part II relies in large measure on the extensive calculations of Hans A. Bethe, professor of physics emeritus at Cornell.

The BMD panel benefited substantially from the advice and suggestions of Alfred Brenner, Ashton Carter, Sidney Drell, William Durch, David Hafemeister, Donald Hafner, Raymond Garthoff, Robert Siemann, Walter Slocombe, and Peter Zimmerman. The ASAT panel was aided by Robert W. Buchheim, Abram Chayes, Daniel Duedney, William J. Durch, Donald Hafner, Spurgeon Keeny, Walter Slocombe, and Herbert F. York.

This book project was conceived and edited by John Tirman of UCS. Peter Clausen, UCS senior arms analyst and a member of the BMD panel, authored Part I and was instrumental in the compilation of the book. Peter Didisheim and Charles Monfort of UCS aided us with research. The diligent editorial assistance of Pat Skantze and Nancy Stockford was indispensable to the completion of this project as well. Special thanks also go to Jon Lomberg and his assistant Joy Alpert for the outstanding illustrations.

Anne Freedgood of Vintage deserves a medal for patience and, we hope, foresight.

Howard C. Ris, Jr.
Director, Nuclear Arms Program,
Union of Concerned Scientists
Cambridge, Massachusetts

policy analyst, Department of Energy and Central Intelligence Agency.

Richard L. Garwin, IBM Fellow at the Thomas J. Watson Research Center; member, President's Science Advisory Committee (1962–65) and (1969–72); member, Defense Science Board (1966–69).

Noel Gayler (Admiral, USN, Ret.), former Commander in Chief, U.S. Forces in the Pacific; former Director, National Security Agency; former Assistant Chief of Naval Operations (Research and Development).

Richard Ned Lebow, Professor of Government and Director, Peace Studies Program, Cornell University; former Professor of Strategy, National War College; Scholar-in-Residence, Central Intelligence Agency.

Carl Sagan, Professor, Astronomy and Space Sciences, and Director, Laboratory for Planetary Studies, Cornell University.

Victor Weisskopf, Institute Professor Emeritus, Massachusetts Institute of Technology; former Director-General, European Organization for Nuclear Research (CERN), Geneva; former President, American Physical Society.

Assistant of Naval Operations (Research and Develo
ment).

Henry W. Kendall, Chairman, Board
Directors, Union of Concerned Scientists; Professor
Physics, Massachusetts Institute of Technology.

Franklin A. Long, Professor of Chemist
Emeritus, Cornell University; former Associate Dire
tor, U.S. Arms Control and Disarmament Agency.

Leonard C. Meeker, member, Board
Directors, UCS; U.S. Ambassador to Romania (196
73); Legal Advisor to the Department of State (196
69).

Carl Sagan, Professor, Astronomy and Spa
Sciences, and Director, Laboratory for Planetary Stu
ies, Cornell University.

Herbert Scoville, Jr., Deputy Direct
Research, Central Intelligence Agency (1955–6
President, Arms Control Association.

John Steinbruner, Director of Forei
Policy Studies, Brookings Institution, 1978–prese
Associate Professor of Organization and Managem
at Yale, 1976–78.

The UCS report on ASATs and the draft treaty v
presented to the Senate Foreign Relations Commit
on May 18, 1983, by Kurt Gottfried, Richard L. G
win, and Noel Gayler.

CONTENTS

PART I

Introduction

1:

THE EVOLUTION OF SPACE WEAPONS

The invention of nuclear weapons was the most dramatic technological breakthrough in military history. The destruction of Hiroshima, just six years after the discovery of nuclear fission, inaugurated the nuclear era. In 1945 only the United States could make atomic weapons, and the military muscle built to defeat fascism appeared ready to enforce a Pax Americana: the U.S. armed forces controlled the seas and airways that any potential attacker would have to cross. America was totally secure.

The United States did not rest on its laurels. The nation's scientific knowledge, industrial skills, and unmatched resources were quickly exploited to expand the U.S. nuclear arsenal with growing numbers of hydrogen bombs, intercontinental bombers, and nuclear-tipped missiles launched from land or sea. Yet despite this stream of ingenious military innovations, American security declined precipitously because the Soviet Union, though devastated by World War II and technologically inferior to America, acquired its own formidable nuclear force in less than twenty years. The Russians showed that they had the will and the means to duplicate Western technical advances.

The United States maintained unquestioned nuclear superiority throughout the 1950s and 1960s, but the political utility of that superiority was difficult to see. The Soviet Union converted Czechoslovakia into its puppet, suppressed revolts in Hungary and Poland, and supported the invasion of South Korea and insurrections in Southeast Asia. Still, an obsessive drive toward more sophisticated weapons impelled both nations, as it does today, to accumulate nuclear arsenals whose dimensions already exceeded any rational political or military requirements long ago.

The result of that obsession has been two decades of living under the threat of "mutual assured destruction," the guarantee that a crushing nuclear attack by one superpower will spark a crushing nuclear retaliation in return. This demonic pact is not the product of careful military planning; it is not a policy or a doctrine. Rather, it is a fact of life. It descended like a medieval plague—momentous, inexorable, and somewhat mysterious. And even as the specter of atomic annihilation settled over the political terrain of East and West, it became common to regard the threat of mutual suicide as neither logical or moral. But beyond that bare consensus, there were sharply divergent views of how to end the nightmare of "The Bomb."

Opinions are no less divergent today. Powerful groups within the governments of both superpowers believe that unremitting competition, though short of war, is the only realistic future; they believe that aggressive military exploitation of whatever technology offers is critical to the security of the nations they serve. Still others have placed faith in radical steps—novel political proposals, revolutionary technological breakthroughs, or both.

President Reagan's Star Wars initiative—dramatically introduced in a televised speech on March 23, 1983—belongs to this last category. In calling on the scientific community "to give us the means of rendering these [nuclear] weapons impotent and obsolete," the president was urging a technological revolution that would enable the United States to "intercept and destroy strategic ballistic missiles before they could reach our own soil." His words envisaged a people liberated from deterrence, "secure in the knowledge that their security did not rest on the threat of instant retaliation." With unassailable hope, the president said: "It is better to save lives than to avenge them."

The vision of a perfect defense is immensely attractive, but it raises complex questions. Can Star Wars eliminate the threat of nuclear annihilation and end the arms race? Or is it an illusion that science can re-create the world that disappeared when the nuclear bomb was born? Will the attempt to install space defenses instead precipitate a nuclear conflict that could not be confined to space? These questions have intertwined political and technical strands. They must be examined carefully before the United States commits itself to the quest for a missile defense, because such a commitment would carry the nation—and the world—across a great divide.

If the president's vision is pursued, outer space could become a battlefield. An effective defense against a missile attack must employ weapons operating in space. This now peaceful sanctuary, so long a symbol of cooperation, would be violated. And the arduous process of arms control, which has scored so few genuine successes in the nuclear era, would also be imperiled— perhaps terminated—by the deployment of weapons in space.

The competition for Star Wars weapons is now in its embryonic stages. The United States and the Soviet Union are developing and testing anti-satellite weapons (ASATs) with modest capabilities. Much more lethal weapons, able to destroy satellites that warn of nuclear attack and others that command U.S. nuclear forces, will be built if the space arms race is not slowed down.

Anti-satellite warfare, though less exotic and far less threatening to peace, is still part and parcel of the space-based missile defense demanded by President Reagan. Determined pursuit of the latter will surely foreclose attempts to restrain the former. Similarly, negotiated constraints on ASAT weapons would seriously handicap the development of missile defenses. In this sense, space weapons form a seamless web, offering a choice between two very different paths: a major national commitment to struggle for military dominance on the "new high ground," or a broad agreement with the Soviets to ban space weapons.

The belief that science and technology can relieve America and Russia of the burden of nuclear deterrence has gripped many policymakers and the public alike for nearly forty years. Sadly, this belief has usually propelled both nations toward more weapons-building, not less. And the technological revolutions so earnestly sought by successive presidencies have undermined American security when the Soviets copied our lead.

Perhaps the most virulent form of this marriage of technological hope and ideological fear is the search for the perfect defense, the protective shield that would re-create the days before atomic weapons menaced every hour. With the advances in space technology and the growing reluctance to seek political accommodations, it has returned again.

DETERRENCE AND DEFENSE: THE ABM DEBATE

Two approaches to defense against nuclear weapons have been pursued. One attempts to protect people or other targets against the effects of nuclear explosions, and is reflected in civil defense programs and the "hardening" of missile silos and military command posts. The other seeks to intercept and destroy the nuclear "delivery vehicles"—missiles and bombers—before they reach their targets. Because of the immense destructive power of nuclear weapons, interception is the far more attractive strategy—if it can be accomplished.

Both superpowers invested in air defenses in the 1950s, but by the end of the decade the ballistic missile was replacing the bomber as the mainstay of nuclear arsenals. Since then, any hope of blunting a nuclear attack has rested on a solution to the problem of ballistic missile defense, or BMD. Research on this problem was under way even before the missiles were deployed in large numbers, but until the mid-1960s BMD remained an obscure and esoteric issue on the fringes of strategic policy. This situation changed dramatically in 1967 when the Johnson administration decided to build the Sentinel anti-ballistic missile (ABM) system. (The terms ballistic missile defense, or BMD, and anti-ballistic missiles, or ABM, are used interchangeably.) This decision sparked an intense controversy that largely dominated the debate on U.S. nuclear policy until 1972,

Figure 1. *Growth in Soviet and American Nuclear Arsenals.*
SOURCE: *Scientific American,* November 1982.

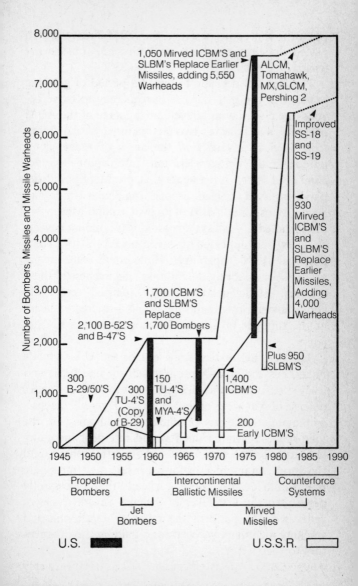

Number of Bombers, Missiles and Missile Warheads

1,050 Mirved ICBM'S and SLBM's Replace Earlier Missiles, adding 5,550 Warheads

ALCM, Tomahawk, MX, GLCM, Pershing 2

Improved SS-18 and SS-19

930 Mirved ICBM'S and SLBM'S Replace Earlier Missiles, Adding 4,000 Warheads

1,700 ICBM'S and SLBM'S Replace 1,700 Bombers

2,100 B-52'S and B-47'S

Plus 950 SLBM'S

300 B-29/50'S

300 TU-4'S (Copy of B-29)

150 TU-4'S and MYA-4'S

1,400 ICBM'S

200 Early ICBM'S

| 1945 | 1950 | 1955 | 1960 | 1965 | 1970 | 1975 | 1980 | 1985 | 1990 |

Propeller Bombers

Jet Bombers

Intercontinental Ballistic Missiles

Mirved Missiles

Counterforce Systems

U.S. ▬   U.S.S.R. ▭

when the superpowers signed the ABM Treaty, which placed drastic restrictions on both sides' missile defenses.

The Sentinel decision followed a period of growing pressure in the U.S. defense bureaucracy to move beyond the research and development stage of the ABM program, and reflected two factors in particular. First, technological advances in the areas of radar, computers, and high-acceleration interceptor missiles convinced ABM proponents that production and deployment were justified. Second, the Soviet Union had begun to install an ABM of its own around Moscow—the so-called Galosh system—and was building new air defenses that appeared to some observers to have a potential ABM capability. While there were strong grounds for doubting the military effectiveness of these systems, sufficient uncertainty existed—especially about Soviet motives and intentions—to create unease at the thought of a Soviet monopoly on missile defenses.

The Sentinel system grew out of the U.S. Army's Nike-Zeus and Nike-X programs of the late 1950s and early 1960s, and was designed to provide an "area" defense of American cities.[1] It was a "layered" defense, employing two types of nuclear-armed missiles: the long-range Spartan, which would intercept incoming warheads before they reentered the atmosphere; and the Sprint, an interceptor for use inside the atmosphere that would destroy those warheads that successfully penetrated the first layer of defense. Several types of radar were to perform the tasks of identifying and tracking incoming warheads and guiding the interceptors to their targets.

The Sentinel decision raised a storm of controversy

in which American scientists played a key role.[2] Critics of ABM deployment pointed to the technical complexity of missile defense and the inherent advantages enjoyed by the offense given the size of the superpowers' nuclear arsenals and their destructiveness against centers of industry and populations. The critics argued that the ABM had fatal vulnerabilities and could be overwhelmed by a determined Soviet attack. In particular, the large, exposed radar installations vital to ABM systems had little chance of surviving a nuclear attack and were susceptible to radio blackout from nuclear explosions, including the defense's own nuclear interceptors. The system's questionable ability to cope with large numbers of targets simultaneously and to discriminate between real warheads and decoys meant that it could also be defeated by a saturation attack. Because in a population attack the cost-exchange ratio between defensive and offensive weapons heavily favors the offense, the Soviet Union could readily afford to offset whatever level of defense the United States deployed. By simply enlarging its ICBM force, the Soviets could ensure defeat of the defense by exhausting America's supply of interceptors.

These criticisms tarnished the credibility of the Sentinel ABM, and discredited the system as a defense of the American public against a Soviet nuclear attack. Questions about the strategic wisdom of ABMs were equally damaging. Here the case against ABM was all the more telling because it drew directly from the prevailing doctrine of strategic stability.* Of particular

---

*The word "strategic" in these discussions—strategic stability, strategic doctrine, and so on—refers to strategic weapons, generally meaning intercontinental weapons. They include intercontinental ballistic missiles (ICBMs), submarine-launched ballistic missiles

significance were two principles that loomed increasingly large in the thinking of Secretary of Defense Robert McNamara during the 1960s: assured destruction and the action-reaction phenomenon.[3]

The concept of assured destruction made a virtue of necessity. It accepted as a fact of life the vulnerability of both superpowers to nuclear devastation. But deterrence resting on the threat of such devastation had two saving graces. First, it put a finite limit on each side's needs for nuclear forces, since only a few hundred retaliatory warheads would threaten "unacceptable" damage to a nuclear aggressor. Second, assured destruction could serve as the basis for a stable nuclear peace, because mutual vulnerability and the certainty of retaliation deprived both countries of the incentive to launch a nuclear first strike that would be fatal to the attacker as well as the victim.

According to this view, vulnerability of populations and invulnerability of retaliatory forces made for stability. Conversely, an attempt by either superpower to protect its population or to develop counterforce weapons designed to attack the other's nuclear forces would be destabilizing. Either of these actions would erode the assured destruction capability of the adversary, undermining mutual deterrence by creating the possibility of a successful first strike.

In this light, a system like the Sentinel ABM—or the Soviet Galosh—was clearly destabilizing. Such weapons were defensive in name only, given the threat they represented to the adversary's deterrent and the contri-

---

(SLBMs), and long-range bombers (such as B-52s). They are thus differentiated from "theater" forces, which are confined to an area like Europe, and "tactical" weapons, which are typically confined to a battlefield.

bution they made to a possible first-strike capability. Ironically, the dubious technical efficacy of these ABM systems made them even more provocative. An imperfect defense might be quite useless to the victim of a well-coordinated first strike, but quite effective in shielding the aggressor from the victim's "ragged" retaliatory strike.

Another notion gaining currency in the 1960s was that of the action-reaction syndrome—to the action of ABM deployments would be the reaction of an accelerated offensive arms race. Since neither the Soviet Union nor the United States would tolerate a serious erosion of its ability to retaliate against the other, each could be expected to compensate for the other's defenses by adding new offensive forces. The hope of stopping and reversing the arms race would be lost.

In light of these considerations, McNamara's eventual endorsement of the Sentinel ABM in September 1967 was understandably hedged and ambivalent. In a speech delivered in San Francisco, McNamara made an impassioned case *against* ABM, emphasizing the action-reaction syndrome and the "mad momentum" of the nuclear arms race. At the end of the speech, however, he announced the decision to proceed with a "thin" Sentinel deployment to protect U.S. cities, not from a Soviet attack, but rather against a much smaller (then nonexistent) Chinese threat. This anti-Chinese rationale was less a coherent strategic approach than an attempt to appease the pro-ABM forces in the United States while minimizing the provocation to the Soviet Union. In fact, McNamara's policy served neither purpose successfully. The Army viewed the decision as a foot in the door; once deployed, the system could be "thickened," or expanded to provide coverage against larger threats. The Soviets could hardly fail to recognize this potential as well, nor could they dismiss Sentinel as irrelevant to their own planning.

The intense domestic debate that followed McNamara's decision focused on the technical characteristics of Sentinel and the strategic implications of ABM in relation to the Soviet Union. Critics drew heavily on McNamara's own arguments to discredit the Sentinel system. Meanwhile, the plan to base nuclear-tipped Sentinel interceptors near major cities gave the issue additional political volatility and inspired a vigorous grass-roots opposition movement.

The Nixon adminstration, inheriting this unpromising situation in January 1969, decided to reassess the Johnson-McNamara ABM policy. The result was a reorientation of the Sentinel program (which was renamed "Safeguard") toward the defense of ICBM silos rather than cities. The change from population defense to silo defense was motivated by a number of considerations. As a matter of domestic politics, the new administration hoped the shift away from cities would dampen public opposition to ABM deployment. Strategically, there was growing concern about the vulnerability of American missiles to a "counterforce" attack—an attack against military facilities—as a result of the Soviet Union's deployment of the huge SS-9 ICBM. Protection of American "Minuteman" ICBM silos in preference to cities was also in keeping with the logic of stable deterrence. By reducing the vulnerability of U.S. retaliatory forces to a Soviet first strike, the Safeguard ABM system would in principle be stabilizing: it would strengthen deterrence, whereas the Sentinel system of population defense threatened to erode it.

The shift to missile defense was also attractive because, in comparison with population defense, it is a far easier mission. Since only a small number of ICBMs need to survive a first strike to assure retaliation, even a highly porous ABM might be adequate for this task. Moreover, some missile sites can be selectively and more heavily protected, leaving some undefended altogether. In contrast, the defense of cities requires virtually an impermeable nonselective shield—both because cities are much "softer" targets than missile silos and can thus be destroyed by even a very few warheads, and also because all cities would have to be defended.

Still, the Safeguard system proved as controversial as its predecessor, and the ABM debate raged on. Critics pointed out that while the system's rationale had changed, the technology had not; the Sentinel, having been designed for city defense, was poorly suited to the defense of missile sites. And though the distinction between protecting populations and protecting missiles was clear enough in theory, in practice it was far less apparent. Safeguard remained a layered, area-defense system, and as such could not be confined unambiguously to a silo-defense role. Any deployment of the system would have to be regarded by the Soviet Union as the potential base of a future population defense; some of the support for Safeguard actually derived from a similar view. The apprehensions about ABM being destabilizing and fueling an action-reaction process persisted.

In August 1969, Congress narrowly approved funding to begin production of the Safeguard ABM, with Vice President Spiro Agnew breaking a 50-50 tie vote in the Senate. Over the next two years, the program retained this precarious grip on survival, increasingly on the strength of its perceived value as a bargaining chip in the U.S.-Soviet Strategic Arms Limitations Talks (SALT) that began in November 1969 in Geneva. In 1972 the two superpowers reached agreement of indefinite duration on a treaty to restrict ABM deployments in both countries in conjunction with a five-year "interim agreement," known as SALT I, which placed limits on offensive nuclear forces.

The ABM Treaty limited each superpower to two ABM complexes, one dedicated to the national capital and the other protecting ICBM missile silos.* Each ABM complex permitted could contain a maximum of a hundred interceptor missiles. In 1974 the two countries agreed to a protocol reducing the number of permitted sites to one each. Consistent with the emphasis of their respective ABM programs at that time, the United States chose to protect a Minuteman missile base near Grand Forks, North Dakota, while the Soviets retained the Galosh defense around Moscow.

The provisions of the ABM Treaty were tailored to prevent either country from deploying a full territorial defense or laying the groundwork for such a defense. To that end, the treaty allows the improvement of permitted ABMs only within well-defined limits and places tight restrictions on the development of new types of ABM systems. It forbids the development, testing, or deployment of ABM systems, or even components, that are mobile and land-based, or based in space, at sea, or in the air. In addition, it prohibits the deployment of so-called exotic ABMs based on technologies or physical principles other than interceptor missiles and radars.

The ABM Treaty marked a conceptual turning point

*See Appendix A.

in the nuclear relationship between two superpowers. It signified an acknowledgment of deterrence based on mutual vulnerability, and of the action-reaction relationship between ABM and offensive nuclear forces. Ironically, however, the treaty failed to prevent the most far-reaching and damaging manifestation of the action-reaction process—the emergence of multiple independently targetable reentry vehicles, or MIRVs.

MIRV technology was pioneered by the United States in the 1960s as a means of multiplying the firepower and target coverage of ICBMs. It enabled a single ICBM to carry several reentry vehicles, each containing a nuclear warhead and guided to a separate target after release from the parent missile. The key role anticipated for MIRVs was the penetration of Soviet defenses in the event that ABMs proved technically proficient enough to jeopardize American targeting plans.

What began as a hedge against an ABM breakthrough soon acquired a life of its own. The initial American flight testing of MIRVs was scheduled to occur in August 1968, just as the superpowers were agreeing to enter into the SALT negotiations. In theory, then, there was an opportunity to halt both MIRV and ABM in a package agreement that would sharply curtail the momentum of the arms race. After all, if widespread ABM deployments could be averted, MIRV would be unnecessary. By the same token, if Soviet MIRVing could be forestalled, the survival prospects of the U.S. Minuteman force would be greatly improved without the need for the Safeguard ABM. The logic of such an agreement was compelling, but it fell before the political and bureaucratic imperatives of the American MIRV program.

Despite efforts in Congress to promote a joint moratorium on MIRV testing, the United States proceeded with the program. Later, in the SALT negotiations, the Nixon administration decided against seriously pursuing restraints on MIRVs. By this time the Soviet interest in controls on MIRVs had also diminished, since such controls would have frozen the large American lead in MIRV technology. As a result, the 1972 SALT agreement on offensive forces established ceilings on missiles but not warheads, leaving the way open for a massive increase in nuclear weaponry by both countries over the ensuing decade.[4]

The missed opportunity to halt the development of MIRVs was doubly ironic. Not only did the ABM threat fail to materialize, but the MIRVing of the large Soviet ICBMs led eventually to the increased vulnerability of American land-based missiles that has so preoccupied U.S. defense planners in recent years. Just such a boomerang effect was predicted at the time, in unheeded warnings conveyed by American scientists to senior government officials. Belatedly, there is now a strong consensus in the defense and arms control communities that a prime objective of U.S. policy should be to put the MIRV genie back in the bottle.

THE ARMS RACE ACCELERATION

During the 1970s the arms race continued apace as both countries deployed MIRVed missiles and the Soviet Union drew even with the United States in nuclear might. While the numbers of delivery vehicles stayed roughly constant following the SALT agreement, the MIRVing of ICBM and submarine-launched missiles almost tripled the number of strategic warheads targeted by the superpowers against each other. By the end of the decade, U.S. warheads had increased from around 4,000 to 9,000, and Soviet warheads grew from less than 2,000 to about 6,000.

Equally important was the *qualitative* dimension of the arms race, particularly in the development of increasingly accurate missiles by both countries. These more accurate weapons were designed for counterforce strikes against missile silos and other "hardened" military targets. By 1980 the United States was deploying a new Minuteman warhead accurate to within some 300 meters of its target at ranges up to 8,000 kilometers, and was developing the ten-warhead MX missile with accuracy of about 100 meters.* The Soviet Union, after lagging well behind the United States in this area for many years, was moving toward comparable accuracies.

This quantitative and qualitative escalation of the nuclear arms race in the 1970s was accompanied by a significant evolution in American strategic policy. Increasingly, McNamara's concept of assured destruction gave way to a more elaborate concept of deterrence, one emphasizing the need for *options* other than all-out retaliation. The desirability of such options had long been accepted and was incorporated into nuclear targeting plans in the 1960s. It was formally recognized by NATO in the late 1960s with the adoption of the flexible response strategy for the defense of Europe. During the 1970s, however, U.S. policymakers em-

---

*Throughout this book, the metric system of measurement is used. From time to time the reader will be reminded of the equivalent weight or distance in the English system. A few that are used frequently include: one kilometer (1 km) = 0.62 miles; one meter (1 m) = 1.09 yards or 3.28 feet; one gram (1 gm) = 0.035 ounces; one kilogram (1 kg) = 2.2 pounds.

braced a version of this strategy that progressively blurred the distinction between deterrence and actual warfighting.[5]

The movement toward warfighting began with President Nixon's doctrine of selective nuclear options and continued with the Carter administration's so-called countervailing strategy. It reached its culmination with the Reagan administration, which effectively equates deterrence with the ability to conduct and "win" a nuclear war. "Should deterrence fail and strategic nuclear war with the USSR occur," the Pentagon's current five-year plan states, "the United States must prevail and be able to force the Soviet Union to seek earliest termination of hostilities on terms favorable to the United States."[6]

The shift from assured destruction to warfighting has profound implications for the numbers and types of nuclear forces needed and, implicitly, for the ABM question that had ostensibly been settled by the 1972 treaty. If assured destruction is no longer the yardstick for nuclear planning, the most persuasive reason for limiting nuclear forces has vanished. The new strategic doctrine calls for ever larger and more diverse forces tailored to a variety of detailed battle scenarios and capable of asserting "escalation dominance"—the ability to respond and prevail at any level of conflict. Moreover, while assured destruction fostered a view of the superpower nuclear balance as essentially stable and impervious to all but drastic changes in numbers, the warfighting doctrine resurrects the idea of meaningful nuclear "superiority." It attaches great importance to numerical disparities between the United States and the Soviet Union, not only in overall forces but in each category of weapons.

By all indications, the Soviet Union has never accepted the notion that nuclear war can be limited and controlled. The Soviets have made it reasonably clear, both by their statements and their deployments, that they intend to respond massively in the event of a serious nuclear exchange. In the face of this, and the vulnerability of the U.S. command and control apparatus, there is little rationale for detailed warfighting plans.

The new doctrine justifies a virtually unlimited proliferation of nuclear forces, subverting the idea that restraints on ABMs would halt the offensive arms race. This continuing arms race, in turn, threatens to erode support for the ABM Treaty, which had encouraged the hope that more serious constraints on offensive weapons would soon be forthcoming. "If an agreement providing for more complete strategic arms limitations were not achieved within five years," U.S. negotiator Gerard Smith said at the time of the ABM Treaty signing, "U.S. supreme interests could be jeopardized. Should that occur, it would constitute a basis for withdrawal from the ABM Treaty."[7]

The *types* of weapons called for by the warfighting strategy also signal problems for the treaty. The trend toward counterforce targeting and high accuracy increasingly puts land-based missile silos at risk of a first-strike preemptive attack, thus reviving one of the main arguments on behalf of ABM systems—that they could protect silos. Warfighting scenarios also suggest possible new roles for ABM systems in limiting damage or protecting command and control centers during a protracted nuclear conflict.

Despite the gradual movement toward warfighting doctrine, the ABM Treaty remained uncontroversial during the 1970s. Indeed, the United States deactivated the Safeguard ABM at Grand Forks in 1975, declining even to deploy what the treaty permitted. The U.S. Army's ABM program reverted to a purely research and development operation, aimed at identifying new technologies for defending hardpoint targets. In particular, the program began to explore ABM defense of the proposed MX missile when an invulnerable basing scheme for the missile failed to emerge.

It was the drastic change in the political climate at the end of the decade—both in U.S.-Soviet relations and in American domestic politics—that ultimately cleared the way for a revival of the ABM debate. The collapse of detente following the Soviet invasion of Afghanistan and the failure of the United States to ratify the 1979 SALT II agreement seriously wounded the arms control process. The election of Ronald Reagan in 1980 brought to power a group ideologically hostile to arms control, convinced of Soviet bad faith, and committed to a major U.S. nuclear buildup to reverse what it saw as a trend toward Soviet superiority. The arms control talks of the 1970s, in the view of the new administration, had lulled the United States into what amounted to unilateral disarmament while the Soviet Union relentlessly forged ahead with a miltary buildup. This was a highly skewed version of recent history, in view of the huge U.S. warhead buildup during the 1970s, which was actually larger than the Soviets', but it was politically potent. The barrage of accusations against the arms control process inevitably exposed the ABM Treaty—the most visible symbol of that process —to a formidable attack. There were early hints from the new administration, reinforced by the prominence it gave to the so-called window of vulnerability facing U.S. land-based missiles, that ABM deployment would receive serious consideration. In a clear departure from its predecessors, the Reagan White House did not treat the 1972 treaty as sacrosanct.

Still, in the strategic modernization program presented by the president in October 1981, the prevailing tone on ABM remained one of caution and technical skepticism. The Defense Department noted that ballistic missile defense

> is not at the technological stage where it could provide an adequate defense against Soviet missiles. For the future, we are not yet sure how well ballistic missile defenses will work; what they will cost; how Soviet ballistic missile defenses—which would almost certainly be deployed in response to any US missile defense system—would affect U.S. and allied offense capabilities; and what would be the political ramifications of altering the ABM Treaty.[8]

An even greater note of caution was struck by the President's Commission on Strategic Forces (the Scowcroft Commission) in its report on the MX missile and related nuclear policy questions: "At this time," the panel concluded, "the Commission believes that no ABM technologies appear to combine practicality, survivability, low cost, and technical effectiveness sufficiently to justify proceeding beyond the stage of technology development."[9]

THE STAR WARS INITIATIVE

Against this background, the president's Star Wars speech on March 23, 1983, appeared to come from out of the blue. His appeal for a major national commitment to ABM was unprecedented in its technological optimism. In calling for a defense so perfect that it would replace the policy of deterrence and "render nuclear weapons impotent and obsolete," the president was questioning not only the previous emphasis of the U.S. ABM program, but the whole foundation of postwar nuclear strategy.

This goal had two immediate implications for the type of defensive system to be pursued. First, a "terminal" defense would no longer be adequate. Instead, it would be necessary, in Secretary of Defense Caspar Weinberger's words, to "engage ballistic missiles and warheads along their entire launch-to-impact trajectories."[10] In particular, the emphasis would be on the interception of Soviet missiles during their "boost" phase—the first few minutes of their flight—before the release of multiple warheads and decoys, and while the rocket and its flame present a good target. (The idea of an Astrodome defense is frequently invoked to describe the hoped-for impermeable ABM, but the appropriate image is that of a dome over the Soviet Union, preventing its missiles from getting out, rather than a dome over the United States to prevent them from getting in.) Second, a boost-phase ABM would require the invention of exotic directed energy weapons that could intercept missiles across vast distances almost instantaneously. These weapons would have to be based in space, or placed there on warning of an attack, to command a view of Soviet missile fields.

The president's unexpected turn precipitated a scramble within the defense bureaucracy to catch up with the new policy. (Even the manager of the Pentagon's directed energy programs, Major General Donald Lamberson, was caught off guard: on the afternoon preceding the Star Wars speech, he was giving the Senate Armed Services Committee a decidedly pessimistic view of the ABM potential of space-based laser weapons.) Following his March 23 address, the president ordered an intensive research and development effort with the "ultimate goal of eliminating the threat posed by nuclear ballistic missiles," and established a panel under the direction of former NASA chief James C. Fletcher to map out a technical strategy for reaching that goal. A second panel—chaired by Fred Hoffman of the California think tank Panheuristics—was directed to study the political and strategic ramifications of the policy. Both groups reported to the White House in the autumn of 1983 with relatively optimistic assessments. In early 1984, Mr. Reagan issued a presidential directive and a proposed budget to launch what was called the Strategic Defense Initiative, or SDI. A new office was created under the Secretary of Defense to run the program, and Lieutenant General James A. Abrahamson was named Star Wars Czar.

The Strategic Defense Initiative is not a wholly new effort: it groups together a number of existing research and development programs. What is new is that these programs are now explicitly aimed toward a comprehensive defense against ballistic missiles and given a priority that is reflected in their budgets and timetables. The SDI identifies several key technology areas—including directed energy weapons, surveillance and tracking, and battle management—and calls for an expenditure of about $26 billion over five years to "provide the evidentiary basis for an informed decision on whether and how to proceed into system development" by the early 1990s.[11]

Although the administration characterizes the SDI as simply a research program, the scale of effort envisaged and the presidential imprimatur with which it was launched stretch the usual meaning of that term considerably. The program calls for technical demonstrations in each of the key technology areas, including space tests of tracking and detection systems. "These demonstrations," the Pentagon's top scientist, Richard DeLauer, told the Congress, "are not small items. They're very expensive and they're extensive and we intend to do them."[12] They may also bring America to the edge, if not over the edge, of the ABM Treaty's prohibitions on the development and testing of space-based ABM systems or components, although the administration denies any near-term intention to abrogate or seek amendments to the treaty.

Impressive as the proposed SDI funding is, it is dwarfed by the cost of actually building and deploying a space-based ABM system. According to DeLauer, "When the time comes that you deploy any one of these technologies, you'll be staggered at the cost." In the same testimony, DeLauer cautioned against excessive optimism and loose talk about the prospects for ultimate success, which he said are dependent on breakthroughs in eight key technologies, each "equivalent to or greater than the Manhattan Project," which produced the first nuclear weapons.[13]

As these statements suggest, the SDI has not evoked a uniformly enthusiastic response within the defense community. Nor has the administration conveyed a consistent vision of the program's objectives or a coherent sense of how SDI fits in with overall U.S. strategic and arms control policies. Instead, the period since the president's March 1983 speech has been replete with mixed signals and conflicting testimony, a clear reflection of internal disarray. Such confusion is not surprising in view of the radical nature of the initiative in its original form and the fact that it was articulated almost entirely outside the normal channels of policy formation and scientific advising.

Administration statements on the SDI reflect a recurring tension between the original, uncompromising vision of a "thoroughly reliable and total" missle defense (in Weinberger's words) and a more modest defense capable of intercepting some fraction of Soviet missiles. While the first version is periodically reaffirmed by senior officials, the second has dominated much of the administration's testimony on the Strategic Defense Initiative. The report of the Hoffman panel, for example, devoted most of its analysis to carving out strategic rationales and missions for partial or "intermediate" systems. It emphasized the protection of U.S. missiles and other military targets rather than population centers in order to strengthen rather than transcend the strategy of deterrence: "U.S. defenses of limited capability can deny Soviet planners confidence in their ability to destroy a sufficient set of military targets to satisfy enemy attack objectives, thereby strengthening deterrence."[14] Similarly, Richard DeLauer testified that the SDI "efforts do not seek to replace proven policies for maintaining the peace, but rather to strengthen their effectiveness in the face of a growing Soviet threat."[15]

Such statements are sharply at odds with the president's original appeal. Attempting to reconcile the tension, officials have described an evolutionary process of improvement in which limited defenses are a step toward a total system. But this approach leaves important questions unanswered. The first is how nuclear stability is to be maintained during the transition "from here to there," given that the two versions of the program—silo defense and total defense—rest on funda-

mentally different premises, one consistent with traditional concepts of deterrent stability and the other not.
The second concerns the implications of the initiative
for offensive nuclear forces: will the United States protect and supplement these forces, or prepare the way
for phasing them out? As the president noted in his
March 1983 speech, "if paired with offensive systems,
[defenses] can be viewed as fostering an aggressive policy." Yet such pairing is the clearly stated goal of Secretary Weinberger, who told the Senate Armed Services
Committee on February 1, 1984: "If we can get a system which is effective and which we know can render
their weapons impotent, we would be back in a situation we were in, for example, when we were the only
nation with the nuclear weapon and we did not
threaten others with it."

How does the SDI relate to arms control objectives?
Here the administration has turned the action-reaction
syndrome on its head and suggested that progress on
defenses would facilitate reductions in offensive forces
by convincing the Soviets of the obsolescence of their
ICBMs. Arguing for early demonstration of key ABM
technologies, presidential science advisor George Keyworth has put this remarkable notion most plainly: "If
I were a Soviet planner, I would quickly put two and
two together and realize that an important part of the
technology for an ABM system was well in hand.
. . . Such a demonstration would pressure the Soviets
to take our arms reduction proposals much more seriously than they do now."[16] But here, too, there are
ambiguities. Is the objective to eliminate the threat
posed by Soviet nuclear forces or simply to promote a
restructuring of those forces—away from the large
land-based missiles that threaten U.S. ICBM silos—in

keeping with traditional deterrence notions and the administration's own policy in the Strategic Arms Reduction Talks (START)? The situation was made murkier still when the Scowcroft Commission warned in March 1983 that the ABM Treaty was critical to arms control success and that the president should exercise "extreme caution" in moving forward with the SDI.[17] A year later, however, Dr. Keyworth was telling Congress that the administration sees "the investigation of strategic defense options as an absolutely vital catalyst to real arms control."[18]

This confusion mirrors a deeper ambiguity as to how the SDI relates to the overall superpower relationship. The administration appears undecided as to which of two incompatible conceptions of U.S.-Soviet relations will govern its approach. One maintains that there is a mutual U.S.-Soviet interest in moving from an "offense-dominated" to a "defense-dominated" world. The two countries would negotiate a new arms control regime to facilitate this shift, and officials have even suggested that the United States might share defensive technologies with the Soviet Union. The other model regards the SDI as a new dimension of U.S.-Soviet rivalry and assigns it a key role in the reassertion of American supremacy. Strategic defenses are seen as a lever to force the Soviets to submit to arms control on U.S. terms, and as a way of breaking the current nuclear stalemate. The second model is both nostalgic, seeking to restore the strategic superiority once enjoyed by the United States, and futuristic, looking to space as the decisive arena of the superpower competition and the most promising place for a technological triumph over the Soviet Union. In this view, the military control of space is imperative, and it is here that the questions of missile defense and anti-satellite warfare become intertwined.

THE ASAT CONNECTION

The leading edge of the arms race in space is anti-satellite weaponry. Unlike exotic space-based missile defenses, ASATs exist today. They are being developed and tested by both superpowers. Yet there is a close link between the two, in strategy as well as technology. Neither can be effectively developed or controlled in isolation from the other.

Satellites are two-faced. Whether they display the aggressive or peaceful side of their character can quickly change as the world moves from peace through crisis to war.

Satellites have become essential to military communications, reconnaissance, intelligence gathering, and navigation. They form a large part of the central nervous system that warns of nuclear attack and controls strategic forces. Military satellites are force multipliers because they enhance the effectiveness of both the nuclear and the conventional forces that they serve. As a result, satellites would be very tempting targets once conflict begins, or was about to begin. In this light, the emergence of anti-satellite weapons may seem inevitable.

At the same time, satellites serve stability in peacetime and crisis. They provide mutual reassurance about the two countries' activities and capabilities, including compliance with arms control agreements. Early-warning satellites add to the deterrence of nuclear attack. Command, control, and communications satellites would be essential to containing an incipient U.S.-Soviet conflict and preventing escalation. These peace-keeping functions of satellites create a joint interest in granting them sanctuary from attack. In addition, the United States has an even stronger incentive to protect satellites, because it is more dependent on them for intelligence gathering and global military communications than the Soviet Union is.

Coupled with the technical complexities, these considerations have until recently moderated U.S. interest in ASAT weapons. As early as the Eisenhower administration, the attraction of being able to attack Soviet satellites was judged to be outweighed by the risks of an ASAT arms race that would put American satellites at risk of attack. Nevertheless, the United States was the first to develop and test rudimentary anti-satellite systems during the 1960s and early 1970s—a fact often ignored in the current space weapons controversy.[19]

The earliest U.S. ASATs employed nuclear-armed interceptor missiles operating from bases in the Pacific and had only a limited capability against low-orbit satellites. The use of a nuclear warhead in these systems was a liability, since it threatened collateral damage to U.S. satellites. The first such weapon, based on the Nike-Zeus ABM system, was deployed between 1963 and 1967. Another, using an intermediate-range ballistic missile, was deployed until 1975 and tested sixteen times. Meanwhile the Soviet Union began testing an orbiting ASAT weapon in 1968 but suspended testing three years later.

The "modern era" of ASATs began in 1976, when the Soviet Union resumed testing and the Ford administration approved the development of a new and more capable anti-satellite weapon. President Carter reaffirmed this decision and awarded a contract to the

Voight Corporation for development of a small, air-launched ASAT, designed to be carried by an F-15 jet and to destroy its target by high-speed collision.

Part of the rationale for the U.S. system was a concern that Soviet ocean-reconnaissance satellites had become a potential threat to the security of American naval forces. More important, the new ASAT was conceived as a bargaining chip to induce the Soviet Union to agree to a mutual ASAT ban. American leverage was assumed because of the superiority of U.S. ASAT technology. In the somewhat hyperbolic words of one Carter administration official, "I don't think the Soviets want to force us into the anti-satellite business, because with the programs we have under way, we could clean up the skies in twenty-four hours."[20]

Negotiations on ASAT arms control were held in three sessions during 1978 and 1979. A number of issues surfaced during the talks, including the problem of defining the weapons or actions to be controlled and the perennial question of verification. Some progress was reportedly made toward at least a partial ASAT agreement, but the talks adjourned inconclusively in the wake of the invasion of Afghanistan and the subsequent breakdown of U.S.-Soviet relations.

The Reagan administration declined to seek a resumption of ASAT talks and replaced the two-track approach, which regarded the U.S. weapon as a bargaining chip, with a one-track policy committed to testing and deployment. In response to congressional pressure to resume negotiations with the Soviets, the administration issued a report on March 31, 1984, which portrayed the verification problems of ASAT control as essentially hopeless. The White House also questioned whether it was in the military interests of the United States to restrict these weapons:

No arrangements or agreements beyond those already governing military activities in outer space
have been found to date that are judged to be in the
overall interest of the United States and its Allies.
The factors that impede the identification of effective
ASAT arms control measures include significant
difficulties of verification, diverse sources of threats
to U.S. and Allied satellites, and threats posed by
Soviet targeting and reconnaissance satellites that
undermine conventional and nuclear deterrence.[21]

Meanwhile the U.S. Air Force conducted the first test
of the F-15 system in January 1984 and planned to
deploy some 112 ASATs beginning in 1987.

The Reagan administration's balancing of the risks
and benefits of anti-satellite development represents a
sharp break with previous policy. Aside from its pessi-
mism about verification and other specifics of an ASAT
regime, the adminstration's position appears to be
motivated by two factors. First is the attraction to the
development of these weapons for their own sake.
ASATs are seen as pivotal in the emerging superpower
struggle to control space. "The policy for the first time
really recognizes the need to be able to control space as
a military environment," says a senior Pentagon official. "It directs the kinds of activities, including the
development of an operational ASAT . . . that may be
necessary to mount space weapons in the future if that
appears to be in the national interest."[22]

The second motive is to lay the stepping-stone between ASATs and space-based missile defense systems.
Technologically, a large overlap between the two exists.
U.S. programs in directed energy weapons, space surveillance and tracking, and related areas are essentially
generic, with potential applications to either ASAT or
ABM missions. The F-15 ASAT system itself is derived

from the Army's ABM program. The ASAT mission is
far less demanding than missile defense, however, because the targets are more fragile, fewer in number, and
remain in space for months or years rather than minutes. As a result, ASAT development and testing offers
a technologically convenient proving ground for space-
based ABM systems and their components.

This link between ASAT and ABM is legally convenient as well: space-based missile defenses are banned
by the ABM Treaty while ASATs are essentially unfettered. The treaty restricts ASAT programs only in prohibiting interference with satellites that are used to
verify strategic arms control accords.

This loophole was of only hypothetical significance
at the time the ABM Treaty was negotiated, but it now
threatens the continued effectiveness of the treaty's restrictions on development and testing of space-based
ABMs or components. Controls on ASATs would
close the loophole and thereby deprive the Reagan administration of an avenue for embarking on the Strategic Defense Initiative while remaining nominally in
compliance with the ABM Treaty. The importance of
this motive for opposing ASAT negotiations was indicated by George Keyworth, who has advocated testing a ground-based laser in these terms: "It may not
necessarily be the best way for the ASAT mission, but
a geosynchronous anti-satellite capability is important
to test the technology to destroy missiles."[23]

The BMD-ASAT connection was forcefully illustrated on June 10, 1984, when the U.S. Army successfully destroyed a dummy Minuteman warhead over the
Pacific with an interceptor using the same homing technique as the Air Force's F-15 ASAT. The test also
demonstrates that the U.S. low-orbit ASAT capability

is somewhat more potent than the Soviets', since the Army's weapon intercepts more quickly than the Soviet ASAT and its homing technique is more difficult to foil. The objection that the United States could not negotiate while the Soviets enjoyed an ASAT monopoly has therefore been shattered.

The Reagan policy underscores that space weapons are all of a piece. Simply put, the nation does not have the choice of indulging in a quest for Star Wars defenses while holding the line against anti-satellite weapons. Nor can the United States pursue the development of ASATs and still enjoy the protection of a robust ABM Treaty. The approaching crossroads offers only two directions—toward an unrestrained space weapons race or an agreement to ban those weapons.

The reports that follow point unequivocally to the path of negotiations. The technical prospects for anti-satellite weapons and space-based missile defenses are strikingly different: ASATs are clearly workable, though they remain rudimentary at this point, while the chances of reaching the president's goal of effective ballistic missile defense are negligible. But these opposite technical prognoses work together to make a ban on space weapons all the more compelling. It is because anti-satellite weapons will improve, at great peril to U.S. security, that they need to be halted now. And it is because Star Wars defenses hold so little promise, while posing great risks, that we are well advised to relinquish the illusion they so temptingly embody.

PART II

Space-Based Missile Defense

2:

OVERVIEW OF SPACE-BASED MISSILE DEFENSE

The President's Strategic Defense Initiative, a "comprehensive and intensive effort" with the "ultimate goal of eliminating the threat posed by strategic nuclear missiles," proposes to rely on unborn generations of sophisticated space weapons. According to the secretary of defense, these weapons would provide a "thoroughly reliable and total" defense. We will adopt Mr. Weinberger's words, and refer to the president's goal as *total ballistic missile defense,* or *total BMD.*

Every sane person yearns to escape from the specter of nuclear annihilation. But that consensus still leaves a host of unanswered questions: will these BMD systems, which are still only conceptual designs, provide a total defense of our civilization against the Soviet missile force? That force now carries 9,000 nuclear warheads, each far more powerful than the Hiroshima bomb and able to arrive on U.S. targets within thirty minutes. (The U.S. arsenal is of course equally devastating.) If these defenses of the distant future could protect us totally against today's threat, could they cope with the Soviet strategic weapons of their own era?

What would the Soviets' response be? Would they devote themselves to a similar effort and agree to reduce their offensive nuclear forces? Or would they perceive this new American program as an attempt to nullify Soviet nuclear forces, a supplement to the emerging capacity to destroy Soviet missiles in their silos? If so, would they not respond with a missile buildup and "countermeasures" to confound our defenses, so that they could still destroy the United States (just as the United States can destroy the Soviet Union)? Or would the Soviets not have this option because our defense would be truly total—robust enough to foil any offensive countermove?

The following seven chapters address these questions, examining the proposed BMD systems in the light of the scientific facts and principles that will govern their performance. The analysis will be aided by the information released publicly by the administration's Defense Technologies Study Team, headed by Dr. James C. Fletcher. There is general agreement, shared by the Fletcher panel, that a defense of our population is impossible unless the vast majority of Soviet missiles can be intercepted in the first phase of their flight while their booster engines emit a brilliant flame and before their multiple warheads are released. As a result, the bulk of our attention is devoted to boost-phase defense.

In assessing each BMD system, we first assume that it will perform as well as the constraints imposed by scientific law permit—that targets can be found instantly and that aiming is perfect, that the battle management software is never in error, that all mirrors are optically perfect, that lasers with the required power output will become available, and so forth. Above all, we first assume that the Soviets' forces remain static—that they do not build more missiles or install any countermeasures. Consequently, our initial appraisal ignores the critical question of whether BMD will eventually work as well as it possibly could, and does not depend on classified information.

Even in this optimistic view, our findings concerning the proposed BMD schemes for boost-phase interception are that:

- Excimer lasers on the ground, whose beams would be reflected toward boosters by over a thousand orbiting mirrors, would require power plants that alone would cost some $40 billion.
- Many hundreds of laser battle stations in low orbits, or space trucks carrying kill vehicles, would be required to give adequate coverage of the Soviet silo fields.
- The atmosphere and the earth's magnetic field combine to make particle-beam weapons implausible into the foreseeable future.

The proposal to launch X-ray lasers pumped by nuclear explosions at the time of an attack would require a new fleet of submarines, as there is no suitable base on land close enough to Soviet silos to allow interception in the time available. The laser's soft X ray cannot penetrate the atmosphere and delivers a rather light blow from which the booster can readily be protected. These facts, when combined with the feasibility of shortening the boost so that it ends before the missile leaves the atmosphere, imply that the X-ray laser is not a viable BMD weapon.

Merely the R&D portion of this program has been described by Richard DeLauer as having at least eight components, "every single one . . . equivalent to or greater than the Manhattan Project." The size of the systems and all costs will climb rapidly should the mirrors be imperfect, the time for aiming exceed several seconds, redundancy be desired, and so on. Full costs cannot even be estimated because the proposed technologies are still too immature. It is clear, however, that many hundreds of billions of dollars would be needed.

These findings assume a minimal Soviet reaction to a U.S. missile defense. Yet the Soviets have made it clear that they view the quest for total BMD as an unacceptable threat. They fear that such a BMD system would give the United States the option to strike first—an understandable fear, since Mr. Weinberger has said that he would view a similar Soviet system as "one of the most frightening prospects" imaginable. And the Soviets have heard administration officials speak of space-based BMD as a lever for stressing the Soviet Union's technologically less sophisticated economy.

In the real world, a determined Soviet reaction must be expected. And that reaction is likely to be unconstrained by all existing agreements, because the very testing of our defensive weapons would violate our obligations under the Anti-Ballistic Missile Treaty. The Soviet reaction is likely to include:

- Offensive missiles designed to circumvent BMD, such as submarine-launched cruise missiles that cannot be intercepted from space.
- Fitting new ICBMs with more powerful engines so that the boosters would burn out both quickly and inside the atmosphere. Such an alteration in boosting would stress any BMD system and eliminate the

possibility of interception by kill vehicles and X-ray lasers.

- Cheap decoy ICBMs—boosters without warheads in fake silos—to overwhelm boost-phase interceptors.
- Weapons that would exploit the fact that even a battleship's armor could not protect a space station from quite primitive types of attack.
- Other easily developed countermeasures that would vastly complicate the problem of targeting boosters and warheads.

All these countermeasures would exploit the off-the-shelf weapons and techniques that exist today in contrast to the unproven and exceedingly difficult technologies on which the proposed U.S. defenses would rely. As a result, the Soviet response will be cheaper and far more reliable than U.S. defenses, and available as those defenses emerge.

While the quest for a total defense against nuclear missiles would be endless, the decision to embark would have immediate political impact. The first repercussion has already been heard: President Reagan's rebuff to Soviet overtures to negotiate constraints on anti-satellite weapons—a stance dictated by the plans for a space-based BMD system. The ABM Treaty could not survive if space weapons were continually being developed and tested, and with its demise all constraints on offensive forces would go overboard as well. The impact on NATO would be profound: our allies in Europe would not be protected by an American BMD system, a fact that would inflame existing suspicions that the United States intends to conduct nuclear operations in Europe without risk to itself. Alliance cohesion would erode as Europeans held the United States responsible for exacerbating East-West tensions.

The risk to American survival would mount dramatically were the building of the BMD system ever to begin. This budding system would be exceedingly vulnerable to attack. Nevertheless, its potential capabilities would be overvalued by U.S. adversaries, and its installation could well be perceived as an attempt to disarm the Soviet Union. These circumstances could in themselves provoke open conflict. Furthermore, a space-based BMD system that was not robust enough to fend off a large-scale strategic attack would still pose a grave threat to high-altitude satellites that provide warning of enemy missile launches and command friendly strategic forces.

If America were to pass safely through this hazardous passage, would we reach the promised land where nuclear weapons are "impotent and obsolete"? Not likely. We would then have a defense of stupefying complexity under the total control of a computer program whose proportions defy description, and whose performance would remain a deep mystery until the tragic moment when it would be called into action.

The president and his entourage occasionally argue that we must pursue this quest because the benefits of success outweigh the costs and dangers. That is an argument for a research program only, in strict conformity with the ABM Treaty and thus devoid of danger. Such a program has always had our support. It is needed to protect us from Soviet surprises, and it might uncover concepts that could actually provide a viable defense. But there is an enormous gulf between such a program and a call from the ramparts for a national "experiment" to mount a defense based on untried technologies and provocative doctrines. We have delineated the risks of such an "experiment." At best, the outcome would be a defense of precarious reliability, confronted by offensive nuclear forces designed to circumvent and overwhelm it, and a host of new "anti-BMD" weapons to attack our armada of space platforms that in turn would have to be defended by yet another fleet of anti-anti-BMD weapons.

It is difficult to imagine a more hazardous confrontation. And it is equally difficult to understand how anyone can believe that this is the path toward a less dangerous world. A direct and safe road is there for all to see—equitable and verifiable deep cuts in strategic offensive forces and immediate negotiations to ban all space weapons. If we are to take that road, we must abandon the misconception that nuclear explosives are military weapons, and the illusion that ever more sophisticated technology can by itself remove the perils that science and technology have created. We must instead recognize the overriding reality of the nuclear age—that we cannot regain safety by cleverly sawing off the thin, dry branch on which the Soviets are perched, for we cling to the same branch.

3:

PHYSICS AND GEOMETRY VERSUS SECRECY AND CLAIRVOYANCE

Two prevalent misconceptions must be dispelled before analyzing the technical prospects for space-based missile defense. The first is the belief that complex military systems cannot be assessed without access to highly secret information. The second is that scientists can do anything given enough money. These are related misconceptions; both see science as a somewhat occult activity.

A sound appraisal of the prospects for space-based missile defense *can* be given on the basis of firmly established scientific laws and facts. To a large extent, such an assessment can be understood by inquisitive citizens without specialized knowledge. No one should shrink from forming a judgment on this issue.

Highly classified information is sometimes indispensable to understanding the performance of a particular weapon system. Without disclosures by the U.S. government, the public would know very little about the explosive energy ("yield") of nuclear weapons or the accuracy of intercontinental missiles. Assessing ballistic missile defense, however, does not require such information. In particular, we are evaluating *total* ballistic missile defense—a defense of our society against an armada of some 10,000 nuclear weapons—not merely the defense of highly reinforced (or "hard") military targets, such as missile silos and command bunkers.

To know whether a defense can be expected to protect, say, 20 percent versus 70 percent of our missile silos would require detailed classified data about missile accuracy, weapon yield, and silo hardness. In contrast, a population defense must be virtually leakproof. Even a handful of thermonuclear explosions over our large cities would kill millions instantly, and would disrupt our society beyond recognition. A missile defense must also intercept enemy warheads far from their targets. Interception of warheads as they are dropping onto our cities or other "soft" targets will not do: nuclear charges can be set to explode as soon as the warhead is struck by a defensive weapon, and this "salvage-fused" warhead would still destroy its target if its yield is sufficiently high.[1]

To defend U.S. society totally then, attacking missiles must be intercepted soon after they leave their launch sites or while they are traversing space. Interception means the delivery of a blow to the enemy missile powerful enough to disrupt it in some way. This is precisely where the constraints of geometry and physics enter, for it is only in science fiction that unlimited amounts of energy can be transmitted over arbitrarily large distances against a tiny target moving at great speed.

The real-life problems of missile defense have been studied intensively by the U.S. defense establishment for a quarter of a century, and some of the authors of this book have contributed to many phases of this effort. These investigations have made it clear that a total missile defense must overcome a number of daunting obstacles that involve immutable laws of nature and basic scientific principles. If the attacker sets out to evade and overwhelm the defense, these same laws and principles are, almost without exception, on the attacker's side. Accordingly, to erect a total BMD one must leap over these obstacles by some combination of novel, ingenious measures, and do so with enough of a margin to compensate for the attacker's innate advantage that just one large bomb can destroy a city.

What are these immutable laws of nature and basic scientific principles? A few of the most important examples:

- The earth rotates about its axis and satellites move along prescribed orbits. In general, therefore, a satellite cannot hover above a given spot, such as a missile silo complex in Siberia.
- Even a thin layer of atmosphere absorbs X rays.
- Electrically charged particles follow curved paths in the earth's magnetic field.
- A laser can emit a perfectly parallel pencil of light, but the wave nature of light guarantees that this beam will eventually flare outwards and become progressively more diffuse.
- The earth is round; a weapon must therefore be far above the United States to see a silo in Siberia.

The relevance of these principles to the feasibility of missile defense will become apparent in the following chapters. As will become clear, the analysis does not rely on classified information; the laws of physics and geometry are the essential ingredients.

In assessing any particular proposed system, we will

give it the benefit of the doubt and assume that it performs as well as the constraints of science permit. What is not yet known by anyone, and will usually be veiled in secrecy, is how close the effectiveness of the proposed system comes to its maximum possible value. But this ignorance has no impact on our assessments since, for the sake of clarity, we assume that this limit will be reached.

All of these theoretical BMD systems are exceedingly optimistic extrapolations beyond current state-of-the-art technology. To a large extent, the status of current technology is reported in the open literature, and the Fletcher panel's assessments of the gaps between our current abilities and the requirements for a space-based BMD system, among other evaluations, have been widely reported. Every total BMD system that has been proposed is comprised of a large set of distinct devices. In virtually every instance, existing prototypes for these individual devices perform far below the theoretical limit. So a prodigious gap exists between the current capabilities of the proposed systems and the theoretical limits that are granted in this book. For that reason, it is not possible to make sound estimates of the true cost of these systems, for that would require a level of engineering knowledge that does not exist at either the public or the classified level.

Nevertheless, it is important to gain a rough understanding of the costs that would be involved. Consider the person who has thought of the automobile and wishes to estimate its cost before inventing the internal combustion engine. Knowing how to construct wagons, the inventor devotes considerable effort to estimating the cost of the automobile's body to obtain a lower limit, perhaps an order-of-magnitude estimate. In a similar vein, we rely on the law of energy conservation: if a beam weapon in space must deliver a certain amount of energy to disrupt enemy missiles, that energy must come from a fuel supply. The cost of the whole system, therefore, is certainly far greater than the cost of lifting that fuel into orbit.

A common perception, and one that is often voiced in the debate over missile defense, is that science and technology can accomplish any designated task. That is certainly untrue. The laws of thermodynamics tell us that one cannot build a perpetual motion machine, and the principle of relativity implies that it would be futile to try to design spaceships that move faster than the speed of light. The laws of nature set limits on what human beings can do. Nevertheless, it is true that the advances scored by science and technology have been remarkable and often unpredictable. But none of these advances violated firmly established laws of nature. Furthermore, these breakthroughs employed new domains of physics, as in the development of nuclear weapons, or fundamentally new technologies, as in the invention of radar.

The current proposals for missile defense, however, do not depend on any fundamentally new physics. Rather, BMD concepts, while displaying great ingenuity, rely on devices that exploit well-known principles of physics and engineering. Should new concepts for total missile defense be put forward, the whole matter will have to be analyzed anew.

Public discussion will help lead the nation to the best path toward national security and will help to avoid the worst pitfalls. Such an open debate will not provide the Soviet Union with information or insights that it does not already possess, because Soviet defense analysts are well versed in the scientific and technological principles under examination.

The remarkable scientific advances of the twentieth century share one essential characteristic: they were not opposed at every step by a resourceful and ingenious adversary. Yet the most important factor in the issue at hand is the certainty that the Soviet Union will react vigorously to a massive U.S. commitment to missile defense. The threat that U.S. defenses would face when they first emerge a decade or more from now would be very different from that posed by current Soviet strategic forces. This dynamic character of the threat is ignored by those who draw a parallel between the quest for a total missile defense and the decision to undertake a landing on the moon. They seem to forget that when the Apollo Program was launched we already knew that the moon was not populated by a powerful nation bent on frustrating our mission.

4:

THE ELEMENTS OF A STRATEGIC ATTACK

Before examining the feasibility of defense, we must have an understanding of the nature of a strategic missile attack. In this chapter, the life history from launch to impact of individual missiles of various kinds will be described briefly. With this information in hand we will be able to visualize actual attacks, which are likely to involve a large number of missiles, and gain a first glimpse of the task facing the defense.

The separate elements of a strategic force can readily be described—missiles with certain characteristics, different phases of flight, and so on—but the way that they could be combined to mount an attack cannot be anticipated with any confidence. There are many different scenarios for attacks, from small demonstration salvos to massive first strikes that disarm the victim. If one intends to erect a *total* defense, however, the exact nature of a nuclear attack is practically irrelevant, because one must be able to withstand the full weight of *any* attack the adversary launches.

As will become apparent, a total defense of the

United States against ballistic missiles is only feasible if a very large fraction—perhaps nearly 100 percent—of these missiles can be disabled during their boost phase. For that reason, and because boost-phase interception introduces many of the techniques and problems of any BMD system, the major part of the following analysis focuses on boost phase.

BOOST PHASE

The flight of a land-based ICBM begins with the silo cover sliding back or popping open. The missile is usually ejected from the silo by hot gases, and its journey begins in earnest when the first-stage booster ignites. Somewhat later the first stage falls away and the second-stage engine takes over. If there are further stages (for example, three in all for the MX), this process repeats itself. This first portion of the journey—from the earth's surface to the point where the last stage stops burning—is called boost phase (see Figure 2).

Superficially there is no essential difference between the flight of land- and submarine-based ballistic missiles. But a submarine-launched attack has an important element of surprise: the sites of all Soviet silos are precisely known to the United States, whereas the location of Soviet submarines is not known. The time between launch and impact can be much shorter for an SLBM than for an ICBM—as short as 8 to 10 minutes in contrast to 25 to 30 minutes. If the submarine is relatively close to its target it can send its missile along a trajectory having a lower maximum altitude (a depressed trajectory). Obviously it is far more difficult to mount an effective defense against missiles that start their journey from an unknown point and have a shorter flight time and lower trajectory.

Figure 2. *Phases of Ballistic Flight.* The various phases of a ballistic missile trajectory. Balloon decoys, some concealing actual warheads, are deployed in post-boost phase. Discriminating warheads from decoys is very difficult until decoys burn up in reentry phase. An ICBM attack launched from 1,000 silos could include more than 100,000 decoys.

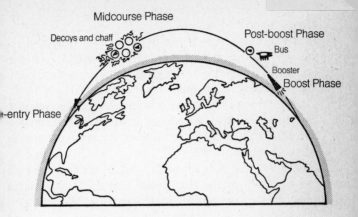

The Fallacy of Star Wars

Boost phase is extremely important to missile defense for four reasons.

First, once boost phase is over, the missile will release a number of warheads. If it faces a BMD system, the missile will also be designed to release a large number of decoys to complicate the task of the defense. Indeed, the very existence of multiple-warhead missiles in today's strategic forces is due to the attempt by the Soviet Union and the United States to construct missile defenses in the 1960s.

Second, the booster flame, similar to that seen on television during civilian space launches, sends out a vast amount of infrared radiation. This infrared light, invisible to the human eye, is almost instantly detected by sensors on satellites tens of thousands of kilometers away. This intense light gives the defender an accurate fix on the location of the target missile. The booster reveals itself like a firefly in a darkened room, while the warheads are as elusive as gnats in the dark. Indeed, it is only in boost phase that the missile emits an intense infrared signal that is easily seen at large distances. Once boost phase is over, one must illuminate the warheads with radars or lasers, and then detect the reflection of the microwaves or the laser light from the warheads. Another post-boost method is to search for the very weak infrared signals emitted by the warm warheads and decoys.

Third, the missile in boost phase is a much larger and more fragile target than the warheads that remain after the boost phase is over.

Fourth, the problems facing midcourse and terminal interception are enormous. It is generally agreed that without a very effective boost-phase kill—90 percent is a figure frequently employed by government officials— no satisfactory defense is feasible.

In short, there is a great premium on interception in boost phase. Every missile that successfully survives boost phase becomes a far more formidable problem for the defense. For that reason, a nation that faces boost-phase missile defense will strive to reduce the time during which its missiles boost. Doing so has two distinct benefits. First, the problems of the defense multiply dramatically if the time for interception is shortened appreciably. Second, some of the weapons that have been proposed for boost-phase interception cannot penetrate the atmosphere, and the altitude at which the booster stops burning is lowered by shortening the boost phase.

The MX is typical of an ICBM with a rather short boost phase: it lasts 180 seconds, and its booster stops burning when it is outside the atmosphere at an altitude of 200 km.* In the absence of missile defenses, there is no need to shorten the boost phase. It is then cheapest to traverse the dense lower atmosphere at modest speed to avoid having to strengthen the missile's structure, and to use a minimum energy trajectory. But the boost phase could be curtailed, and the altitude where burning stops lowered, by spending more money on a faster-

---

*The phrase "outside the atmosphere" actually does not have a precise meaning. The atmosphere's density drops smoothly with altitude. The influence of the atmosphere on various objects and beams depends sensitively on their character, and for that reason some objects (and beams) will be effectively outside the atmosphere at a certain altitude, while others are still inside. Thus a carefully shaped reentry vehicle will penetrate to much lower altitudes than a meteorite before atmospheric drag becomes significant, while X rays and particle beams are depleted by the atmosphere at far higher altitudes than optical beams. As Table 2 in Chapter 5 shows, at 200 km all BMD techniques are unaffected by the atmosphere, so a booster is truly outside it; but at 100 km, it is shielded from many types of BMD interceptors. More details concerning atmospheric effects will be given in due course.

Figure 3. *Ballistic Missile Trajectories.* The flight of missiles can be directed on a depressed or lofted trajectory to make interception more difficult.

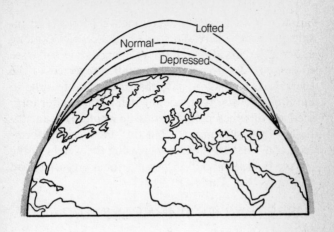

burning and sturdier booster that would burn out inside the atmosphere. Such a missile could fly along either a depressed or minimum energy trajectory (see Figure 3). Missile contractor studies reported to the Fletcher Commission state that it is quite feasible to develop a booster that would finish burning after forty seconds, at which point the missile would have an altitude of only 80 km, and that this enhanced performance could be obtained by increasing the weight of the missile by only about 15 percent for a given payload and range (see Table 1).

DISPERSAL OF WARHEADS AND DECOYS

Most modern ICBMs carry multiple independently targetable reentry vehicles (MIRVs), each of which contains a warhead. When such a missile completes its boost phase, what remains is a so-called MIRV bus. The bus releases its passengers, the warheads, one by one along somewhat different paths to their separate targets, and for that purpose the bus is equipped with thrusters that allow it to make relatively small changes in course. This segment of flight is frequently referred to as the post-boost phase.

If there are missile defenses, the bus would also carry a variety of decoys to compound the task of the defense. For example, the bus can dispense a vast number of very light metallic objects, called chaff, which are designed to reflect radar and confuse the image seen by the defense. Another decoy candidate is a light, multi-layered balloon of metallized plastic film; most of these balloons would be empty, but some would surround warheads. All of them would have the same appearance to radar or an infrared sensor.

Some proposals envisage intercepting ICBMs while their warheads are being dispersed. This option could be frustrated by a technique that suddenly deploys warheads and decoys as soon as boosting ends, while maintaining present targeting accuracy, or by the use of microbuses (see Table 1).

MIDCOURSE AND REENTRY

Once the bus has released all its warheads and decoys, the attacking missile is said to be in *midcourse*. It is actually no longer a single missile: what was one object in boost phase has become a swarm. It is quite reasonable to expect a modern ICBM such as the SS-18 or the MX to release ten or more warheads, a hundred or more decoys, and quantities of chaff, clouds of infrared-emitting aerosols, and other so-called penetration aids. Once midcourse is reached, a thousand silos could readily present the defense with hundreds of thousands of potential targets swathed in clouds of purposely confusing debris. In the vacuum of space, all these objects, no matter how light, fly along ballistic trajectories, just like an astronaut on a space walk. One cannot differentiate the heavy warheads from decoys and chaff by even the most precise tracking. It is also exceedingly difficult to distinguish decoys from warheads by passive observation. In all likelihood, the defender will either have to shoot at both decoys and warheads or actively interfere with both in order to find the heavy warheads. Taken altogether, midcourse interception may be the most daunting portion of missile defense because the problem of target identification is so acute.

When the descendants of the original missile reenter the atmosphere, the heavy warheads mounted on carefully shaped reentry vehicles are exposed because air

Table 1. Times for Boost-Phase and Warhead Dispersal

ICBM	Burnout of Booster time (sec)	height (km)	MIRVing Finished t	h
SS-18 two-stage liquid highly MIRVed	300	400	N.A.	N.A.
MX three-stage solid 10 MIRVs	180	200	650	1,100
MX—fast burn microbuses and decoys and RVs	50	90	60	110
MIDGETMAN —fast burn + decoys 1 RV	50	80	N.A.	N.A.

*Ashton Carter. "Directed Energy: Missile Defense in Space." Washington, D.C.: Office of Technology Assessment, April 1984. The first two entries refer to the most modern components of the Soviet and U.S. strategic forces; the SS-18 is deployed, the MX is tested but not deployed. The last two are designs of ICBMs prepared by the Martin-Marietta Corporation for the Fletcher Panel, under the supposition that a Soviet boost-phase BMD system would require missiles that finish boosting and warhead dispersal as quickly as possible. (RV = reentry vehicle; N.A. = data not available.)

friction tears away the veil of light decoys and chaff. *Terminal defense* is therefore feasible, provided one seeks to protect only hard targets, where interception as close as a fraction of a mile is adequate. A defense that eliminates a portion of the incoming warheads can save a significant fraction of one's missile silos and preserve the capacity for a devastating response. The same terminal defense will not protect a city because a handful of warheads can destroy very large urban areas. Furthermore, incoming warheads can be salvage-fused, set to detonate as soon as they sense interception. Above a certain quite low altitude (which depends on the yield of the weapon), the resulting blast would not destroy a silo or hardened command post. On the other hand, a nuclear explosion quite far above a city can devastate it.

CRUISE MISSILES

A number of delivery systems can evade even a perfect ballistic missile defense. As mentioned earlier, low-trajectory SLBMs would probably not be subject to midcourse or boost-phase interception. Nuclear devices smuggled into the adversary's country certainly evade defenses. Perhaps the most important challenge to BMD, however, is that posed by cruise missile technology.

A cruise missile is a small, ground-hugging pilotless airplane that can carry a nuclear warhead over distances of thousands of kilometers. It flies to its target by measuring the altitude of the overflown terrain with on-board radar and matching that altitude against a map stored in its computer's memory. An accuracy sufficient to threaten hard targets is attainable, though the time from launch to impact is much greater than it is for ballistic missiles. Cruise missiles capable of penetrating into the Soviet Union are already on our B-52 strategic bombers and are now being deployed on the ground in Europe by NATO. Both superpowers could fire cruise missiles from submarines to strike both civilian and strategic targets far inside their adversary's borders, from unpredictable launch points.

None of the space-based defense systems that are being considered can touch cruise missiles. That is not their purpose. Until a virtually perfect shield against cruise missiles is developed, there is no such thing as a *total* missile defense. No one doubts that a significant number of U.S. strategic bombers (not just their cruise missiles) could penetrate the highly touted Soviet air defense system to deliver their high-yield bombs on target. Cruise missiles are far harder to detect with radar than much larger, higher-flying airplanes, and as the so-called STEALTH techniques—which will make aircraft less visible to radar—develop, cruise missiles will become even more elusive. Since they are unmanned, a high attrition rate is quite acceptable. These characteristics make it very difficult to envisage a shield against air- and sea-launched cruise missiles that would protect our population.

STRATEGIC ATTACKS AND ELEMENTS OF TOTAL MISSILE DEFENSE

The elements of a total missile defense include several technologies and tasks that relate separately to each stage of the strategic attack but are not weapons per se. The first important function is that of early warning of attack. Early-warning systems have for some years been an essential part of the U.S. strategic force. These systems employ geostationary satellites with sensors to detect the telltale infrared emissions from rockets in boost phase. Warning would be available immediately after the attacking rockets had left the lower atmosphere.

The next task of a defense would be to provide a threat assessment: determining the precise number of missiles, their positions and, to the extent possible, their identities. The defense could use sensors on aircraft, on satellites, or on "popped-up" platforms. Target "acquisition" and tracking would quickly be under way. Here the task is to distinguish each object in the "threat cloud," and to begin the process of determining its trajectory by a sequence of measurements of position and velocity. At the same time, the defense would attempt to discriminate between the objects in the threat cloud in an effort to weed out decoys and other false targets.

Computers in the BMD battle-management system would use the tracking and targeting information to assign interceptors and beam weapons. The tracking information is required to provide positions and other data about potential targets in the case of homing interceptors, and aim points for beam weapons.

Releasing the interceptors or firing the beam weapons is the signal for starting the next task: finding out what happened. This is the job of damage assessment. For those cases where the beams or interceptors went astray, a determination of what went wrong is necessary. Then, if time permits, there is a second round of weapons firing, and a third, and so on, until time runs out. During all of this the defense would be under attack and must be able to defend itself.

5 :

BOOST-PHASE INTERCEPTION

If one is to intercept missiles in boost phase, one must decide where to place the interceptor and how to carry out the interception. These are related questions for the interception technique is constrained primarily by the distance from the defensive weapon to its target. We begin by analyzing the advantages and drawbacks of different basing modes. This is followed by brief descriptions of the various space weapons that have been proposed: infrared, ultraviolet, and X-ray lasers, kill vehicles, and particle beam weapons. The next five sections of this chapter provide a closer look at some of the deployment schemes that have been put forward for such weapons. Readers who are not interested in such technical discussion can, without loss of continuity, skip these sections and proceed to the final section on countermeasures. Indeed, it is far more important to understand the countermeasures; their efficacy and political implications do not depend on the detailed properties of the various BMD systems under discussion. The countermeasures rely on *existing* technologies and

quite simple aspects of orbital motions and are therefore easier to understand than the proposed BMD systems themselves.

BASING: ORBITING BATTLE STATIONS VERSUS POP-UP INTERCEPTION

Since we cannot station our defenses on Soviet soil, and
Soviet silos are not in the line of sight from U.S. soil,
attacking a Soviet missile in boost phase must be done
from space. Such weapons would either be in space
before the attack begins, or be launched into space after
our early-warning satellites announced that an attack
was under way.

If our defensive weapons are to be there and
waiting, they must be on satellites—so-called *orbiting battle stations.* To minimize the distance to the
enemy's missile silos, one would hope to choose an
orbit just above the edge of the atmosphere and to
have enough satellites so that at least one will be close
to each silo. The properties of satellite orbits are determined by Newton's laws of motion, however, not
by defense planners, and the laws of motion require a
satellite in such a low orbit to revolve about the earth
in about one-and-a-half hours. Since the earth itself
revolves, the satellite is not above the same point on
the earth every time it completes a circuit (see Figure
4). As a result, a battle station in a low orbit is "on
station" near the opponent's missile field only once or
twice a day.

Can one avoid such chronic absenteeism? Yes, but at
a large price. There is one special orbit, above the equator, where the motion of the satellite is precisely in step
with the rotation of the earth. A satellite in this *geostationary* orbit is 36,000 kilometers (22,000 miles) above

Figure 4. *Target Coverage from Orbiting Laser.* This figure shows regions accessible to attack by satellite in an orbit that passes over the North and South Poles (a polar orbit). Most Soviet silos are close to the Trans-Siberian Railway, which is shown. Boosters within the circular regions can be attacked at various times by a satellite having an altitude of 1,000 kilometers and equipped with a weapon with a range of 3,000 kilometers. The ground tracks of two successive passes are shown, as well as three "snapshots" of the target area; two which are 13 minutes apart on the first pass, and the other 94 minutes later when the satellite is on its next pass.

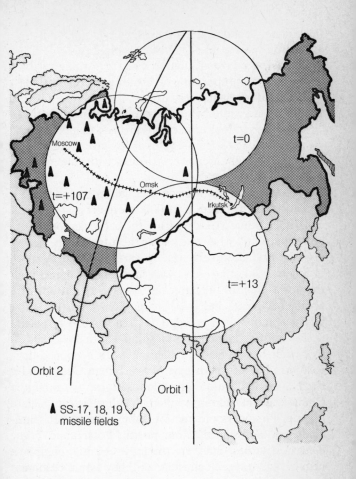

Moscow

Omsk

Irkutsk

t=0

t=+13

t=+107

Orbit 2

Orbit 1

▲ SS-17, 18, 19
missile fields

the equator, or some 39,000 kilometers (24,000 miles) away from Soviet missile silos (see Figure 5).

In brief, the laws of motion and the turning of the earth present proponents of orbiting battle stations with two unpleasant alternatives:

1. A very large number of stations in low orbit. In this case, the small portion of this armada that is within a view of enemy missile fields at any given time must carry enough firepower to deal with the whole ICBM attack by itself.

2. The creation of a weapon that can intercept at the enormous distance of 39,000 kilometers.

This leads one to ask whether the battle stations can be "popped up" when one knows the attack is on. Now another hard fact intervenes: the earth is round. A silo in Siberia cannot be seen by an interceptor popped up from Alaska until the latter has risen to an altitude of about 3,000 km, and by then the Soviet missile will have had more than enough time to end its boost phase.

Can one find launch sites close enough to Soviet silos to permit boost-phase interception with a popped-up weapon? The northern part of the Indian Ocean and the Norwegian Sea are possible locations; two others, China and Pakistan, are not politically feasible. This pop-up mission would require submarine launch but could not be assigned to our present Polaris and Trident submarines. They are the most essential component of our strategic deterrent, and they would become vulnerable if they were not free to roam the world's oceans. So a pop-up missile defense requires a new missile-firing submarine fleet in addition to the interceptors themselves, and probably a fleet of attack submarines and surface vessels to protect the new BMD submarines.

WEAPONS CHARACTERISTICS

All boost-phase interception must be carried out at long distance. Hence it is essential to transmit a blow to the enemy booster with a projectile that can travel quickly. The highest velocity attainable is the speed of light (300,000 km per second). Laser beams, which move at that speed, and beams of atoms or electrons, which are nearly that fast, would be ideal if they could be made intense enough to cause damage at such large distances. Such devices are called directed energy weapons.

A laser emits a beam of light composed of rays that are almost perfectly parallel. (Figures 6 through 10 provide an introduction to the physical principles that underlie lasers.) Several types of lasers are candidates for BMD weapons. The most promising seem to be chemical lasers that emit infrared light, excimer lasers that emit ultraviolet light, and a laser pumped by a nuclear explosion that emits X rays. Free electron lasers, which emit visible light, are also under consideration. (The term "optical laser" will refer to lasers that emit light in the infrared, visible, or ultraviolet portions of the spectrum.)

The wavelength of the radiation emitted by these devices is important. The wavelength of infrared light is longer than that of visible light, while ultraviolet is shorter. It is customary to measure wavelengths in microns (or micrometers), where one million microns is equal to one meter. The characteristic wavelength of visible light is one-half micron. The wavelengths emitted by the chemical and excimer lasers are 2.7 and 0.3 microns, respectively. X rays have vastly shorter wavelengths (0.001 to 0.0001 microns), and must be treated separately.

Figure 5. *Satellite Orbits.* Three types of orbits used by military satellites. The geosynchronous orbit *(b)* has an altitude of 36,000 km and remains at a fixed point above the equator, moving with the rotation of the Earth. A highly elliptical orbit *(c)* rises to as much as 40,000 km above the Northern Hemisphere and dips to less than 1,000 km near the Southern Hemisphere. Low-earth orbits *(a)* are at altitudes from 150 to 2,000 km.

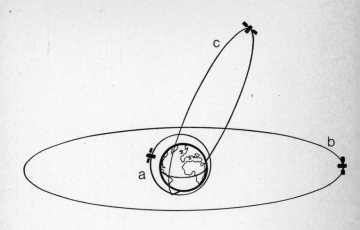

Figure 6. *Depiction of Light Waves.* Light is a wave-like motion of electric and magnetic forces, and the same is true of X rays. Two quantities characterize any wave motion: the wavelength *(w),* which is the distance between successive crests (or troughs), and the amplitude *A,* which gives the height of a crest, as indicated in (a) and (b). The waves shown in (a) and (b) have the same wavelength, but (a) has half the amplitude of (b), the wave in (c) has one-third the wavelength of those in (a) and (b), and its amplitude is 80 percent that of (a). A light wave carries energy at the velocity of light along with the wave itself. The energy is proportional to the square of the amplitude: if we call the energy of wave (a) one unit, (b) and (c) carry 4 and 0.64 energy units respectively, because $(0.8)^2 = 0.64$.

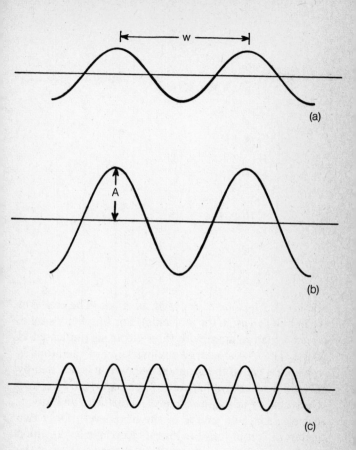

(a)

(b)

(c)

Figure 7. *Emission of Light by an Atom.* The emission of light by an atom (or molecule). For simplicity's sake, we consider an atom with three electrons (indicated as dots). The lowest energy configuration of the atom as a whole is called the ground state, which is denoted by G, and it will be in that state if not disturbed. In G two electrons are in the lowest level available to an individual electron, and one is in the next level. (Only two electrons can fit into the lowest electronic level, which is why G is the ground state.) An excited state E of the atom is formed by lifting one electron into the upper electronic level. The excited state is not stable, however. The atom returns to the stable state G when the electron falls back into the lower level. In doing so, it emits light. The wavelength of this light is uniquely determined by the energy difference between E and G: the larger the difference, the shorter the wavelength.

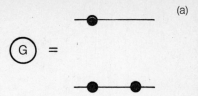

(a)

G =

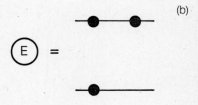

(b)

E =

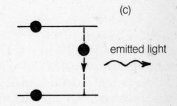

(c)

emitted light

Figure 8. *Spontaneous and Stimulated Emission of Light.* If the excited atom E is in isolation, it will after some time spontaneously emit light with equal probability in all directions. If the excited atom is illuminated with an intense light wave, however, it will be stimulated to radiate light rapidly in exactly the same direction as the illuminating wave. This occurs only if the illuminating wave has precisely the same wavelength as the emitted wave. This process of stimulated emission is the essential ingredient of the laser.

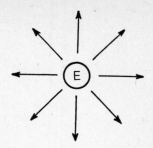

a) spontaneous emission

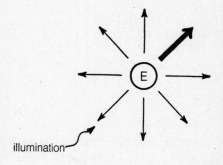

illumination

b) stimulated emission

Figure 9. *Conventional Light Emission, as by a Fluorescent Tube.* The tube is filled with a gas of atoms, most of which are in the ground state *G*, while a small fraction populate the excited state *E*. It is then very unlikely that light emitted spontaneously by one atom will strongly illuminate another excited atom before the latter emits light. (Indeed, since most atoms are in the ground state, the radiated light will, on average, be reabsorbed if the density of gas is increased.) As a consequence, the tube emits light in all directions with equal intensity, and the excited atoms do not act as amplifiers for the light from other atoms.

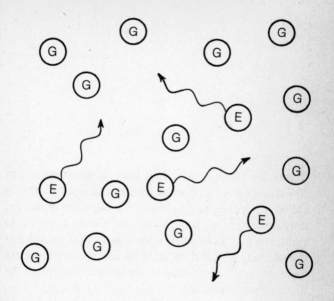

Figure 10. *Laser Action.* In a laser, more atoms are in the excited state E than in the ground state G; this is called a population inversion. For the sake of clarity, only three excited atoms are shown. Going from left to right, the first atom emits a light wave that illuminates the second, which then adds its energy to produce a wave of larger amplitude in the same direction as the illuminating wave, and this is repeated yet again by the third atom. In short, through repeated stimulated emission the laser acts as an amplifier for the light emitted spontaneously by the first atom. In an actual gas laser, the atoms are in a cylindrical arrangement with reflecting end plates. Light that travels parallel to the axis of the cylinder undergoes multiple reflection and therefore illuminates excited atoms repeatedly. Amplification occurs only for light moving along the cylinder's axis; because of repeated reflection from the mirrors, that is the only direction in which the "chain reaction" shown in the sketch can be maintained for a large number of atoms. For laser action to begin, something must be done to produce the population inversion, and if the laser amplification is to continue, that inversion must be maintained even though atoms are returning to their ground state whenever they emit light.

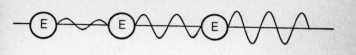

Figure 11. *Outward Flaring of Light Beam.* The wave nature of light prevents optical instruments from concentrating their light into an arbitrarily small area at a large distance. This is illustrated here for the case of a (parabolic) mirror that, were it not for that wave nature, would send out a perfectly parallel beam to infinity from a light source S. (In the case of actual interest to us this source would be a laser.) In the region near the mirror, the waves are almost in perfect step, and the wavefronts—the planes that run through adjacent crests—are almost perfectly flat, as shown, except at the edges, beyond which there is no light! This sequence of parallel flat wavefronts produces the desired parallel beam, whose diameter D will equal that of the mirror. But as the waves travel farther and farther, the edge of the beam expands into the darkness and the wavefronts within the light beam become curved. This leads to the outward flaring of the beam as shown on the right. The distance where flaring becomes appreciable is given by $D(D/w)$ for the device shown here. Once flaring becomes significant, the beam has reduced intensity and lethality, since the energy is spread over an ever-increasing area.

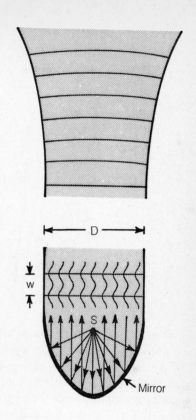

Figure 12. *Collision of a Particle from a Neutral Particle Beam Weapon with an Air Molecule.* A hydrogen atom, composed of a positively charged proton ($+$) and a negatively charged electron ($-$), encounters an air molecule in the upper atmosphere. With very appreciable probability, this will cause the neutral hydrogen atom to disintegrate into its electrically charged constituents, which then follow circular paths in the earth's magnetic field. That field is taken as perpendicular to the plane of the drawing in this illustration. (If the magnetic field is not at 90 degrees to the direction of the hydrogen atom's motion, the electron and proton will travel along helical paths after the disintegration.) For the sake of clarity the electron's circle has been greatly enlarged here and in Figure 13.)

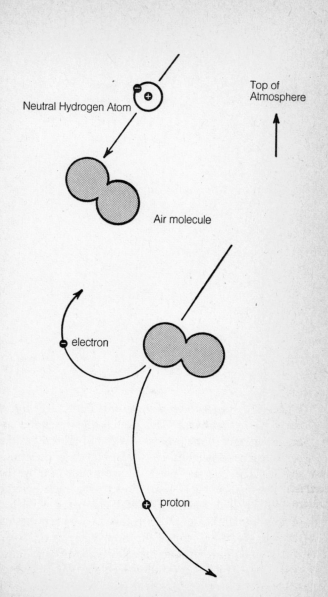

Neutral Hydrogen Atom

Air molecule

electron

proton

Top of
Atmosphere

Figure 13. *Propagation of a Neutral Particle Beam in the Upper Atmosphere.* This sketch illustrates the cumulative effect of the process shown in Figure 12 as the beam reaches down into ever-denser layers of the atmosphere. The charged particles are swept out by the earth's magnetic field and spread over such a large region that their intensity is small compared with that of the initial beam. For instance, after traversing through the first 10 km of the atmosphere, a 100 MeV beam would have protons spread over a width of more than 1 km, which is to be compared with the one meter or so width of the initial beam.

Figure 14. *X-ray Laser.* The X-ray laser is a device that converts a very small portion of the energy released by a nuclear explosion into a beam of X rays. The device consists of a nuclear warhead surrounded by a bundle of very thin metallic fibers. Detonation of the warhead causes the fibers to emit a simple burst of X-ray pulses, directed at enemy missiles, during the minute fraction of a second before the entire device is destroyed by the explosion.

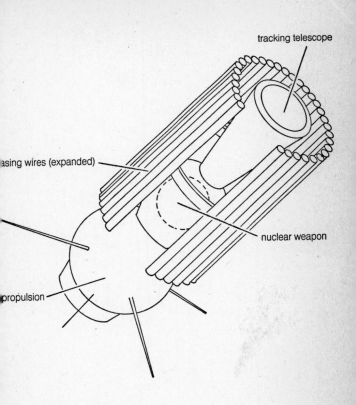

tracking telescope

asing wires (expanded)

nuclear weapon

propulsion

Figure 15. *Chemical Laser.* A laser is a device that emits a beam of light composed of rays that are almost perfectly parallel. In a chemical laser, an infrared beam is produced by the reaction of two chemicals such as the gases hydrogen and fluorine. The beam is focused and aimed by a suitably oriented and shaped system of mirrors.

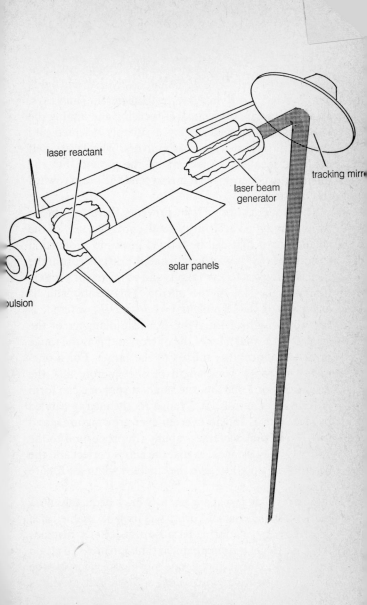

laser reactant

laser beam
generator

tracking mirror

solar panels

pulsion

In a weapon, the beam from an optical laser is concentrated on the target in the same way that one lights a fire with a magnifying glass by focusing the sun's rays. In a space weapon, the task of focusing and aiming the laser beam is carried out by a suitably oriented and shaped mirror or system of mirrors. The laser itself could be located in space or on the ground, but the mirror must be in space if it is to send the beam toward the booster.

The wave nature of light prevents the laser's beam from forming an arbitrarily small spot. The size of the smallest spot that can be formed grows in proportion to both the light's wavelength and the distance from the focusing mirror to the target, and is inversely proportional to the size of the mirror. This relationship is expressed by the formula $d = 1.3 (w/D)R$, where w is the wavelength of the light, d is the diameter of the spot, D is the diameter of the mirror, and R is the range or distance from the mirror to the target. For a one-meter mirror, a wavelength of one micron, and the distance R of 1,000 km, the smallest spot one can form is 1.3 meters across. At a range R, the energy carried by the beam is spread over an ever-growing area, and its effectiveness decreases rapidly (in proportion to the *square* of the distance) even if the aim is perfect and the beam is refocused to give the smallest spot (see Figure 11).

A laser that just manages to work adequately on a battle station in a low orbit will not be usable on a geostationary platform, because the latter's distance from the target is more than ten times greater. To attain such an increase in range, one must either increase the diameter of the mirror, or use a laser that produces light of a shorter wavelength, or both.

All this assumes that the optical system is geometrically perfect. (In technical terms, one says that such a system operates at the diffraction limit.) In reality, if the mirror's shape has imperfections, the spot that it will form will be larger than this diffraction limit, and the energy deposited by it on any given area will decrease correspondingly, making it a less effective weapon. For example, a mirror irregularity of one ten-millionth of a meter will cause a very appreciable degradation in the performance of an excimer laser weapon that uses ultraviolet light. Even if such imperfections could be completely eliminated in manufacture, that might not suffice; this degree of perfection must be maintained while the mirror is reflecting a beam intense enough to damage severely the metallic skin of a booster. Even under the best of circumstances—in a laboratory on the ground—optical systems rarely perform at the theoretical limit. It is difficult to imagine that they would do so under battle conditions in outer space. We nonetheless ignore this note of caution in our numerical estimates.[2] Furthermore, we also ignore the fact that none of the optical lasers has achieved performance levels close to what is required for adequate space weapons. Some of the candidate devices are more than a million times below the power level that would be needed.

The X-ray laser is a device that converts a small portion of the energy released by a nuclear explosion into a beam of X rays. These rays are actually light of very short wavelength, and they travel at the same speed as the beams from ordinary lasers. In contrast to infrared and ultraviolet light, however, X rays are absorbed in the atmosphere and would be useless against a missile whose booster burns out at sufficiently low altitude. The short wavelength leads to another difficulty: X rays cannot be reflected by mirrors. Ordinary optical lasers emit parallel beams because their light has undergone multiple reflections between mirrors that form the end caps of such lasers. Since X rays cannot be reflected, they are not as parallel as the rays of conventional lasers. Consequently, the X-ray laser does not produce a beam concentrated enough to be used from a geostationary platform; it would have to be placed on a low-orbit satellite or popped up. Nor can a mirror be used to aim or focus the X rays on a target, so the entire device must be lined up in the desired direction.

The X-ray laser has one important advantage over all other directed energy weapons: it is by far the lightest of these devices. It exploits the enormous energy release from a nuclear explosion, but only a small fraction of this energy is actually converted by the laser into the X-ray beam.* The X-ray laser is the only device proposed thus far that is anywhere near light and robust enough to be a candidate for a pop-up defense against boosters.

A particle beam weapon would exploit the technology of particle accelerators (atom smashers, in popular parlance). The advantage of a particle beam weapon is that energetic atomic nuclei, such as protons, penetrate to considerable depths even in a metallic structure, and can ruin the semiconductors in the electronic circuits that govern the operation of the missile and the MIRV

---

*Because of this and the large beam spot formed by the X-ray laser, the amount of energy actually deposited on a distant target by the X-ray laser is quite comparable with that from conventional laser weapons, since they have much higher efficiencies and superior focusing.

bus. If such a device is to be an effective weapon, however, major obstacles must be overcome. Only electrically charged particles, such as electrons and protons, can be accelerated or steered toward a target. But such particles then follow a curved path in the magnetic field of the earth and are extremely difficult to aim. On the other hand, neutral particles, such as hydrogen atoms, are not affected by the earth's magnetic field. Devices exist that accelerate and aim charged particles and convert them into a neutral beam before ejecting them. But a device that could produce a beam with sufficient intensity to disable distant targets would weigh in excess of 500 tons. Therefore particle beam weapons appear to be even less promising[3] for boost-phase interception than the other weapons discussed here.* Furthermore, even if such a device could be constructed and placed in orbit, interception could be done only *above* the atmosphere. Otherwise the rapidly moving neutral atoms would collide with air molecules and break up

---

*A typical avant-garde vertical particle beam weapon design assumes an accelerator that produces a 0.1 Amp beam of hydrogen ions having an energy of 100 MeV. A properly compacted guidance computer would be protected from such a weapon by about 15 kg of shielding. If the beam energy were to be raised considerably (say to 500 MeV), the shielding required would become prohibitively heavy. Then an appropriate countermeasure would be a shortened boost phase, for as Figure 13 shows, the atmosphere provides complete protection against particle beams. Another possibility would be to use gallium arsenide semiconductors, which are about 1,000 times more resistant to radiation than currently used semiconductors. It should be noted that a neutral particle beam weapon that is useless against boosters could be a very potent ASAT.

Our rough estimate of 500 tons for the mass of the 100 MeV neutral particle beam weapon takes into account not just the accelerator, but also the beam expansion magnets required to reduce beam divergence, as well as the large-aperture magnets that would aim the hydrogen ions before the extra electron is stripped off.

into electrically charged electrons and ions (see Figure 12). This would re-create a charged beam, which would be fanned out by the earth's magnetic field and be useless as a weapon (see Figure 13).

Small homing projectiles that would damage the booster by direct impact are also envisioned as interceptors. The projectile would carry infrared telescopes to sight the ICBM's booster flame; a set of thrusters, controlled by a small computer that uses the telescope data, would adjust its course to "home" in toward the target.

The best-known kill vehicle is the miniature homing vehicle (MHV), the crucial element in the forthcoming U.S. anti-satellite system. It is a 15-kilogram cylinder, about 30 centimeters in both diameter and length. In its ASAT mode it is carried to high altitude on an F-15 jet and then launched toward its target with a two-stage rocket. Homing on the infrared emission from the target satellite is achieved through the combined action of a set of infrared telescopes, a laser gyroscope that keeps track of the orientation of the spinning cylinder, and a ring of thrusters that encircle the cylinder. The latter are fired on the basis of information from the telescopes, and bring the MHV onto its target. On June 10, 1984, such a vehicle, launched from Kwajalein on an ICBM booster, homed on a dummy Minuteman warhead launched from California, unfurled metallic spokes, and destroyed its target. Since the target was not accompanied by a swarm of decoys and other "penetration aids," it did not demonstrate a BMD capability, though it does establish a U.S. low-altitude ASAT capability.

Such kill vehicles have several advantages over directed energy weapons. They use technology that already exists. The impact of one projectile can destroy a booster, whereas most laser beams would have to dwell on a small spot on a rapidly moving booster for at least several seconds to produce appreciable damage. And the "space trucks" that carry the kill vehicles are less vulnerable to attack than laser mirrors are.

LOW-ORBIT BATTLE STATIONS

We now examine boost-phase interception schemes that would place some of the weapons just described on platforms that revolve about the earth in low orbits.

CHEMICAL LASERS. The most powerful laser that has been devised uses a chemical reaction between hydrogen and fluorine as the energy source. This chemical (or HF) laser produces a beam of infrared light with a wavelength of 2.7 microns. Because of its potency, it is a popular candidate to become a space weapon.

We define a "standard" chemical laser weapon as a device that produces 25 Megawatts (MW) for as long as one pleases and has an optically perfect 10-meter diameter mirror. (The Fletcher Commission calls for a *demonstration* of a 2-Megawatt laser by 1987, so our assumption is very generous.) This 25MW device will produce a circular spot having a diameter of 1.1 meters (or an area of 0.9 square meters) at a distance of 3,000 km and smaller spots with more intense illumination at shorter range.

Assuming that the time available for boost-phase interception is 100 seconds (even though much quicker burnout is achievable—see Table 1), how much energy must be deposited on the booster to disable it? The heat from intense infrared radiation will damage the booster's skin to the point where it can weaken or rupture. The missile fuel will then vent through such defects and produce a catastrophic failure. According to the Fletcher Commission, a booster may fail if its skin absorbs 200 Megajoules per square meter, where one Megajoule is the energy produced by a one-Megawatt power plant in one second (200 MW per square meter is the energy required to evaporate a 7 cm layer of ice). At a range of 3,000 km, our "standard" laser produces a 0.9 square meter spot, onto which it would have to deposit 180 Megajoules of energy to produce the required level of damage. Operating at 25 MW, this hypothetical weapon would have to dwell on the same spot for 7 seconds. As we will see, many weapons will be within range of the silo fields at any time, so by preferentially attacking nearby boosters, the range can, on average, be reduced considerably. Average dwell times as short as 2 seconds might therefore suffice. Assuming that a new target can be selected, assigned, and aimed at instantly, a single battle station could therefore destroy up to 50 boosters during the 100-second boost phase. If there are still 1,400 Soviet ICBMs when this system is deployed, this means that about 30 weapons would have to be within shooting distance of the silo fields at any time. For each weapon of the assumed range, about 10 must be in orbit to have one "on station" for the current geographical distribution of silos. Hence some 300 laser weapons must be in orbit altogether if all of these highly optimistic assumptions are granted.

The cost of putting these lasers into orbit can now be estimated if one knows how much fuel is required to provide the energy emitted by the lasers. Roughly one kilogram of fuel will yield one-half Megajoule of energy in the laser's beam. A 25-Megawatt laser running for 100 seconds will therefore require about five tons of fuel. It costs about $3 million to lift a ton of payload toward the east out of Cape Canaveral into low orbits on the shuttle; lifting into orbits closer to polar, which would be necessary, costs about twice as much. But lifting may be more economical in such a vast program, so the figure of $3 million per ton will be used. The cost of just lifting the fuel for our fleet of 300 lasers is therefore $4 billion. A reasonable estimate for the total weight of the battle station is twice the weight of the fuel, so the cost of lifting the whole armada is about $8 billion. The cost of the laser system would be vastly more than the cost of orbiting the system, just as the cost of building and operating a racing car far exceeds its fuel cost.

While a 25-Megawatt chemical laser equipped with a 10-meter mirror is now well beyond the state of the art, the Fletcher Commission has suggested that eventually it may be possible to build optically perfect 15-meter mirrors.[4] There are also those who claim that a 100-Megawatt chemical laser will be available someday.[5] By then the Soviets could have reduced their ICBM's boost phase to the fifty seconds that the Fletcher Commission says is feasible, and protect their boosters by some combination of techniques to be described below.

These estimates and the number of battle stations are exceedingly optimistic. We have assumed that lasers with very high performance can be developed, that optically perfect focusing mirrors of very large size can be constructed, that aiming is perfect, that the mirror can be turned to a new target instantly, and that the decision as to which laser fires on what booster takes no time and is never in error. Any slippage in this conjectured performance of the system would require a larger number of battle stations and a corresponding increase in cost. If Soviet boosters are eventually hardened beyond the level reportedly assured by the Fletcher Commission—an altogether likely possibility —that too would require a corresponding increase in the size of the battle fleet. Obviously the price of the complete system will be far higher than the cited dollar figures, since we have not counted the cost of research, development, or construction of the battle stations, the ancillary command and control facilities, or the weapons that would be required to protect the battle stations from attack. Given the immaturity of the technologies involved, no one could make reliable estimates of these costs.

Kill vehicles have two major drawbacks that preclude them from serious consideration as boost-phase interceptors. They move very slowly in comparison with laser beams (10,000 times slower), which severely limits their range. Furthermore, they can function only at very high altitudes. This is so because a high-speed object moving through the atmosphere will heat the layer of air next to it, which results in the emission of infrared radiation. But because the kill vehicles utilize infrared signals to home in on ICBM boosters, the infrared signal that it causes by its motion through the air masks its own homing telescope. The phenomena that determine this self-produced infrared background have been studied in connection with the design of reentry vehicles and are quite complex. A rough estimate indicates that a kill vehicle having a shape similar to a reentry vehicle cannot home successfully below an altitude of about 100 km. Boosters that burn out at an altitude of 80 km, therefore, could not be intercepted by kill vehicles. Such vehicles could still attack a MIRV bus, but, as explained earlier, one can design ICBMs that have no bus and release warheads and decoys immediately after boosting is over, or that disperse their warheads and decoys very rapidly at altitudes below 100 km.

In estimating the costs of basing kill vehicles in space, we assume that they can be built to weigh only 5 kilograms, in contrast to the 15 kilograms of the current ASAT homing vehicle. If one mounts this device on a rocket carrying fuel weighing nine times as much as the payload, the kill vehicles would attain velocity of 8 km per second. In the 100 seconds allotted to boost phase, the projectile could cover a distance (its range) of 800 km. Since interception must take place above 100 km, optimum coverage is obtained by basing the kill vehicles in orbits having an altitude of about 160 km. Because their range is so small, not much area on the ground is covered in comparison with that accessible to the laser weapon. As a result, for every "space truck" carrying kill vehicles that is within range of a *particular* silo complex, about 80 trucks must be in orbit somewhere else above the globe. On average, however, two other trucks will be over some other Soviet silo complexes, so for every truck on station, only some thirty more must actually be in orbit. The total weight in orbit is found by multiplying the 50 kg for each kill vehicle, with its rocket, by the number of enemy boosters, and by the absentee factor of 30, and by another factor of about two for the weight of the space trucks themselves. With our standard figure of $3 million per ton to lift into low orbit, it would cost $13 billion to station this whole arsenal of kill vehicles in orbit. As in the case of the lasers, the full cost of the system would be far greater.

If the Soviets modified their ICBMs so that boosting stops at an altitude of 80 km, the kill vehicles would of course be useless as boost-phase interceptors. It should also be noted that the utility of kill vehicles for boost-phase BMD is only marginally enhanced by increasing their velocity. While that would increase their range, it would also raise the ceiling of 100 km below which they could not home effectively, because self-blinding would set in at lower atmospheric density.

GEOSTATIONARY BATTLE STATIONS

Since an enormous number of heavy battle stations are an inescapable affliction of any system that uses lasers or kill vehicles on low-orbit satellites, it is natural to ask whether a more economical system can be constructed by using geostationary platforms 36,000 km high. As noted earlier, the area of the spot a laser beam makes on the ground at a range of 4,000 km will grow by a factor of a hundred when moved from a low-orbit to a geostationary platform, and this hundredfold growth in the beam spot would make the same weapon ineffective in high orbit. On the other hand, a large number of stations uselessly orbiting the earth just to have some small fraction within range of Soviet silo fields is not necessary with geostationary platforms, precisely because they are stationary. If one can solve the first problem—that of the oversized beam spot—then it may make sense to move from low to geostationary orbits.

This may be achieved if a laser that emits light of a shorter wavelength is used. For example, a mirror 15 meters across on a geostationary platform at about

40,000 km from Siberia can produce a one-meter diameter spot if it uses the ultraviolet light from an excimer laser, because that light has a wavelength ten times shorter than that from the chemical laser.

As a result, there have been proposals to put excimer lasers on geostationary platforms. But it is not good enough to have a device that can make a one-meter spot at a distance of 40,000 km. One must also be able to aim it to an accuracy better than one meter (comparable with aiming that is better than 5 inches over the distance from New York to San Francisco). Since the aim point is an infrared booster flare, the geostationary battle station will have to carry an enormous telescope to sight that long wavelength signal, a telescope having a diameter some ten times larger than that of the 10-to-15-meter mirrors used by the infrared lasers in low-orbit battle stations. To convey the prodigious magnitude of a 100-to-150-meter diameter telescope, we point out that the largest telescope in the world (at Mt. Palomar) has a 5-meter diameter mirror.

There is another proposal, advocated by George Keyworth, the president's science advisor, to station the excimer laser on the ground (Figure 16). In this scheme, the excimer beams could be reflected by a geostationary mirror to mirrors in low orbits, which would reflect them again toward boosters rising out of Siberia. This idea seems more plausible than the preceding one, because it has the lasers on the ground and needn't have mirrors as big as a football field floating some 36,000 km above the equator.

Before exploring the technical components of this scheme, it is useful to estimate its electrical power need, which is not sensitive to the details of the interception scheme. With the optically perfect 15-meter mirror

Figure 16. *Ground-Based Laser System.* A ground-based excimer laser would use mirrors stationed in geosynchronous and low-earth orbits. The low-orbit mirrors would be equipped with targeting devices to aim the ultraviolet light from the excimer lasers at boosters rising out of Siberia.

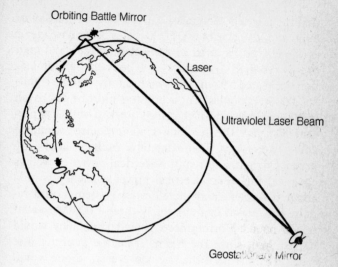

Orbiting Battle Mirror

Laser

Ultraviolet Laser Beam

Geostationary Mirror

that the Fletcher Commission believes can someday be built, and its figure of 200 Megajoules per square meter as the energy required to damage a booster, the total energy required to destroy 1,400 boosters by illumination reflected from geosynchronous orbit equals 200,000 Megajoules. These boosters must be destroyed in 100 seconds, and if the lasers worked with 100 percent efficiency, the total power plant required would be 2,000 Megawatts. Unfortunately, excimer lasers are very inefficient, and require electrical power as well as chemical fuel. The electrical power efficiency is only about 6 percent, and therefore the system would require the output of some thirty-three 1,000-Megawatt power plants. Furthermore, some redundancy would be required, since the beams from the lasers cannot reach the mirrors if the sky is overcast, so one would have to choose several sites to be sure that at least one is clear. There is also substantial absorption of ultraviolet light in the atmosphere, and reflection by the mirrors produces losses. To compensate for weather variations, reflection losses, and atmospheric absorption—to provide a minimum margin of safety—it would be necessary to multiply the power plants available for the lasers by three to ten times. As a result, the excimer laser scheme would require one hundred to three hundred 1,000-Megawatt plants, or the equivalent of 20 to 60 percent of the entire power output of the United States.

One cannot extract such a large amount of power from the commercial grid instantaneously. Nor is it possible to store such a large amount of instantly available electrical energy. Instead, plants designed to deliver such large amounts of power for only a short time would have to be built. A reasonable cost figure for such plants is $300 per kilowatt (as compared with $1,000 to $3,000 per kilowatt for nuclear power plants). The cost of the electric power plants for the laser system would therefore be $40 to $110 billion. If the Soviets shorten the boost phase of their ICBMs to fifty seconds, the system would have to be enlarged and the power plant bill would rise to some $100 to $300 billion.

The system itself poses many complex problems. The first is that when a perfectly plane wave of light is sent up through the atmosphere, what emerges will not be a plane wave but a distorted wave, because of fluctuations in the air density. (This effect is responsible for the twinkling of stars.) When reflected from the geostationary mirror, such a distorted wave will make a spot much larger than that resulting from a perfectly plane wave, even if the mirror is optically perfect (diffraction limited). Dr. Keyworth has intimated that this problem will be overcome by exploiting the new technology of adaptive optics, in which the shape of the mirror is continuously changed by a feedback mechanism to compensate for the disturbances in the incident wave.

We have proposed a simpler scheme for removing the disturbances from the laser wave due to atmospheric fluctuations. In essence, it would use the excimer lasers on the ground as amplifiers for a relatively small excimer laser on the geostationary platform.*

*The high-orbit laser acts as a beacon. First, it would send a plane wave toward the ground-based lasers. Having traversed the atmosphere, the disturbed wave would land on the terrestrial lasers. This disturbed wave would then be used to stimulate the powerful battery of ground lasers. Each member of the battery would thereby have the phase of its oscillations determined by the wave that had already sensed the fluctuations along the optical path in question. When the powerful laser beams from the ground battery emerge above the

Again, this analysis has granted incredibly high levels of performance of these systems. All the caveats concerning performance and cost listed at the end of the discussion of chemical lasers apply here with greater force, since excimer laser technology is much less mature than that of chemical lasers, and because the system has a much more complex architecture.

X-RAY LASERS AS POP-UP INTERCEPTORS

The X-ray laser, invented at Lawrence Livermore National Laboratory and first advocated vigorously by

---

atmosphere, they would, by construction, have precisely those relationships between their phases necessary to form a perfectly plane wave, as if there were no atmospheric fluctuations at all.[6]

The geostationary mirrors would then send their beams to mirrors in low orbits. The latter would be equipped with infrared sighting devices so that they properly reflect the ultraviolet light from the excimer lasers at the rising boosters. The geostationary platform would have to know exactly where its low-orbit mirrors would be on an orbit whose parameters would be known to the desired precision.

As this system will take many years to develop, it is reasonable to assume that by then only fifty seconds will be available for boost-phase interception. If aiming could be done instantly, and the laser beams were so powerful that a booster could be destroyed in just two seconds, about sixty mirrors in low orbit would have to be within firing range at any time in order to kill 1,400 boosters. About ten times that number must be in orbit to ensure coverage of the silo fields. Each low-orbit mirror over the silo fields would have to be fed by a geostationary mirror, so there would be sixty of the latter as well. In principle, the low-orbit mirrors could focus the ultraviolet light to make a considerably smaller spot on the booster, and that would reduce the required laser output. That could not be done, however, with the rather imprecise aim point provided by the booster's flare. An accurate image of the booster itself would be needed. If the booster is highly reflecting, that would be a very difficult task, because a perfectly reflecting cylinder does not send light back toward its source unless the cylinder's axis happens to be perpendicular to the incident direction of the illumination.

Edward Teller, is not a viable BMD weapon for two reasons. First, the Soviets can protect their ICBMs from X-ray lasers totally by shortening the boost phase to the point where burnout occurs inside the atmosphere. Second, even if that is not done, the impact delivered by the X-ray beam is such that one can readily devise schemes for protecting the booster from damage.

According to a Soviet technical publication, the X-ray laser is a device consisting of a nuclear explosive surrounded by a parallel bundle of very thin metallic fibers (some 30 microns in diameter). The explosion brings the surrounding material to a temperature that is found in nature only in the interior of stars. At these extreme temperatures the thermal "glow" is not in the visible part of the spectrum, as in a steel mill, but in the X-ray regime. These "thermal" X rays are sufficiently energetic to disrupt the electronic structure of the atoms in the metallic fibers, and under the right conditions this causes the fibers to lase. The X-ray energy at which lasing occurs is appreciably lower than that of the thermal X rays. Such laser action has reportedly been observed in underground nuclear tests conducted by Livermore.

The intense X-ray pulse from the fiber bundle can be neither reflected nor focused by optical devices in a manner that is useful for the purpose at hand. The geometry of the metallic fibers and the X-ray wavelength determine the angular spread of the emitted beam and the size of the illuminated spot at a distance from the laser. Assuming the fibers are 2 meters long, an X-ray wavelength of 0.001 microns, and a fiber diameter of 30 microns, the laser will make a spot 170 meters in diameter at a distance of 4,000 kilometers. Doubling the length of the fibers produces only a 30 percent reduction in the diameter of the spot. This poor collimation of the X-ray beam has one compensation: it is not necessary to point it with the accuracy required by an optical laser, because at these vast distances the beam spot covers an area much larger than the target. The whole device is destroyed by the explosion, and it emits a pulse lasting for less than one-millionth of a second. In that time, the booster moves a negligible distance, so in contrast to optical lasers, the X-ray laser does not have to track the target's motion.

The X-ray laser can be defeated by fast-burn boosters because the atmosphere is a very effective X-ray absorber. For the X rays in question, penetration to an altitude of about 100 km occurs for a beam that enters the atmosphere from above in a direction perpendicular to the earth's surface. A beam that enters at an angle of 10 degrees to the surface of the atmosphere will penetrate to 120 km. It has been claimed that a sufficiently intense X-ray beam could burn its way through the atmosphere. We have investigated this effect for an intense beam (100 Megajoules per square meter), and find that it adds only 7 percent to the depth of penetration.* These altitudes are to be compared with the 80

*X-ray "burn-through" could in principle be attained if the X-ray pulse were intense enough to almost completely ionize the oxygen and nitrogen molecules in the atmosphere, which could drastically reduce their ability to absorb X rays. We estimate that an X-ray laser having a 1 percent efficiency and an angle of incidence of 30 percent to the horizontal would have to be pumped by a 2.7 Megaton explosion to achieve effective penetration to an altitude of 100 km. This is to be compared with the 300 kiloton explosion that could produce an X-ray pulse having sufficient momentum to damage an unprotected booster above the atmosphere.

km where, according to the Fletcher Commission, it is feasible to complete an accelerated boost.

If we take the optimistic assumption that 1 percent of the yield of a nuclear explosion can be converted into the laser beam, a 300-kiloton explosion could deliver a significant blow to a booster that is outside the atmosphere at distances no more than 4,000 km from the laser. This blow will have two separate effects. First, it will cause the booster to recoil as a whole. Second, it can dent or fracture the booster's skin.

The overall recoil of the booster would, if uncorrected, send the warheads about 1,000 meters away from their intended targets. If the targets were cities, such a deflection would not make much difference, but if they were silos, such an error is of great importance. On the other hand, the sophisticated inertial guidance devices carried by the kind of accurate missiles that can threaten silos would sense the X rays' blow and compensate for the deflection.

X rays of the energy in question penetrate less than one micron into a variety of materials that can be used to coat the booster. And the duration of the X-ray burst is so short that successive layers of the skin cannot be blown off. The resulting pressure wave could, in a careless design, cause the skin to shear at its supports and to damage the booster's interior. The problem of protecting the booster from such a blow bears a certain similarity to that of protecting a cyclist's fragile head in a fall. For example, the booster's skin could be a double layer enclosing a crushable metallic foam. More complex and effective structures for protecting the payload can also be designed.

A shield for the booster could be devised that would prevent the X rays from reaching it altogether. This could be a metallic foil, less than one millimeter thick, which is initially rolled up on a rod like a window shade and carried alongside the booster during ascent through the denser layers of the atmosphere. At an altitude of about 80 km the rod is pushed outward from the booster and the foil is unfurled to form the shield. The orientation of this shield must be chosen so that the X-ray pulse propels the shield in a direction that misses the booster.

Proponents of the X-ray laser envisage the device as a pop-up interceptor. Even setting aside the fact that boosters can be protected from the X rays, the pop-up idea is flawed. Most Soviet silos are in the vicinity of the Trans-Siberian Railway at latitudes of about 55 degrees. The portion of the earth's surface closest to these silo complexes that can be reliably used by U.S. military forces is the Arabian Sea south of Pakistan, at a latitude in the neighborhood of 23 degrees (see Figure 17). The X-ray laser must be lofted to a point in space where it can just see the rising Soviet ICBM while it is still boosting. The distance from the submarine to that point is 1,200 km for a silo due north of the submarine and larger in other cases, assuming that interception takes place at an altitude of about 110 km.

If the laser is lofted by a rocket that uses the most powerful propulsion that can be foreseen (far more powerful than those used by current missiles), the flight time of the laser from the submarine to the point where the laser could initiate interception would be at least 120 seconds. This time would be considerably longer if the lasers were to be launched from a point on land in the Aleutians or Western Alaska, so 120 seconds is the fastest deployment now conceivable for a pop-up laser.

To this two minutes one must add the time required

for the decision to launch. Many elements enter into that time: processing and verifying the signal from early warning satellites that a Soviet attack is under way; acquisition, processing, and transmission to the submarines of enough tracking information so that each submarine can be assigned to a portion of the rising ICBM force, and the firing of the interceptor's booster rockets. According to one authoritative estimate,[7] two minutes are required just to process and verify the data from the early warning satellites. Perhaps a far more complex sequence of decisions and computations can one day be done in a matter of seconds, *provided that no human being has taken part in the whole process.* In any event, the 120 seconds minimum time required for the flight of the X-ray laser is far longer than the 50-second boost phase that should be attainable. Submarines suffer from another related handicap: they cannot fire all their missiles in one salvo. The first of a series of launches from a single submarine would reveal its position (which is by necessity as close as possible to the Soviet Union) and make it vulnerable to prompt attack, while the time between successive shots must be added to the minimum time required for interception.

In conclusion, the X-ray laser offers no prospect of being a useful component of a boost-phase BMD system.

COUNTERMEASURES

All boost-phase interception schemes that have been proposed are vulnerable to a variety of *generic countermeasures*—that is, a spectrum of Soviet reactions that do *not* depend on the details of the schemes, but only on a handful of characteristic features:

Figure 17. *Pop-up X-ray Laser System.* The X-ray laser, pumped by a nuclear explosion, may be launched from submarines in the northern Indian Ocean (or possibly the Norwegian Sea) to be as close as possible to the U.S.S.R. Because of the Earth's curvature, the laser must be fired at a high altitude if it is to have a clear line of sight to the rising ICBM. It would take at least 120 seconds to loft the interceptor from the submarine to the firing point. It is possible to shorten ICBM boost time to 50 seconds.

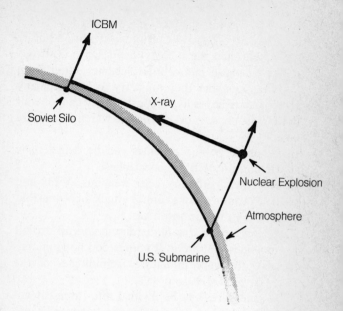

1. Battle stations in space are highly vulnerable to a large variety of relatively primitive attacks, far more vulnerable than the ICBMs they seek to destroy.

2. All boost-phase interception schemes suffer from the weakness that they must try to intercept any object that behaves like a booster; they cannot wait until boost phase is over to decide which objects are fakes.

3. Boost phase pop-up schemes can be defeated by shortening the ICBMs' boost phase.

4. In contrast to ordinary laser weapons, X-ray and particle beam weapons cannot attack a booster that burns out in the atmosphere.

5. The countermeasures under discussion all exploit technologies that are well understood now, in contrast to the very immature technologies of the space-based BMD proposals.

Countermeasures can be divided into three categories: passive, active, and threatening. A "passive" countermeasure protects the attacker's missiles against the defender's weapons, but does not attack or damage those weapons. Examples of passive countermeasures include shortening the duration of the boost phase, and coating a booster to reflect a laser beam, or surrounding the booster with a heat-absorbing layer. An "active" countermeasure is one that interferes directly with the BMD system, or even seeks to destroy its components. For example, satellites belonging to the attacker can project an abrasive material against laser mirrors on a BMD battle station. A "threatening" countermeasure is one that directly exposes the nation that owns the BMD system to a level of threat higher than that faced before it deployed its BMD system. An example of a threatening countermeasure is a massive buildup of true and fake offensive weapons that are specifically designed to exploit the characteristic weaknesses of the BMD system. The classic example is the multiwarhead missile (MIRV), the countermeasure par excellence for the BMD system of the 1960s. While it is true that all successful countermeasures lead to the same result—more nuclear explosions landing on the defender—from a psychological and political perspective the distinction between threatening, active, and passive measures is highly significant.

THREATENING COUNTERMEASURES. Anyone who doubts that a total BMD deployment is perceived as a threat by the other side needs only to listen to Secretary of Defense Caspar Weinberger, who said that if the Soviets were to build a similar system it would be "one of the most frightening prospects" imaginable. A total BMD program in the United States will create an even more vivid nightmare in Soviet minds, because the Soviets are aware that the U.S. edge in technologies such as computing, optics, pointing and tracking, and microelectronics would put them at a disadvantage in a BMD deployment race. Their apprehensions will have been reinforced by George Keyworth, whose public statements suggest that one important underlying motive in pursuing space-based BMD is to force the Soviets into a competition in which they are handicapped.[8]

Under these circumstances, it would be only prudent to expect Soviet reactions that do not rely on ill-understood new technologies and that are certain to be perceived as threatening by the United States. Such a course would not be available to the Soviet Union if the U.S. defensive system was so effective and cheap that

Table 2. Boost-Phase Countermeasures[a]

System	Minimum Altitude of Interception	Passive	Active
Chemical laser in low orbit	0	Harden booster Disguise flame	ASAT
Kill vehicles in low orbit	100 km	Shorten boost* Disguise flame	ASAT
Excimer laser on ground mirrors in space	0	Harden booster Disguise flame	SLBM attack on lasers or surroundings ASAT vs. mirrors
X-ray laser on subs popped up	110 km	Shorten boost* Harden booster	
Particle beams	130 km	Shorten boost*	

ASAT = Anti-satellite weapons—e.g., space mines, pellet swarms
[a]All boost-phase interception can be swamped by cheap fake boosters.
*Fatal passive countermeasures

an offensive buildup would be futile. As we have seen, however, none of the proposed BMD systems comes close to meeting that criterion. On the contrary, even under highly optimistic assumptions, the effectiveness of the defense will be questionable at best, while its cost would be higher than that of simply replicating nuclear delivery systems already in the Soviet Union's inventory.

What, then, is the cheapest, surest, and most threatening Soviet response to an American BMD? The answer is obvious: a massive buildup of offensive weapons and decoys. SALT II and the ABM Treaty would have long been dead letters if a BMD system were being deployed. The United States could not test or deploy such a system without abrogating the ABM Treaty, and the Soviets would not tolerate the limits on their missile force imposed by SALT II if they were about to be faced by a missile shield. As a result, there would be no numerical limits on silos or on ICBMs. Nor would there be the rule in Article XII of the ABM Treaty forbidding "deliberate concealment measures which impede verification by national technical means," so silos would be built under cover to prevent satellite observation during construction. In these conditions, it would be possible to construct many cheap silos and a new generation of fake ICBMs consisting of boosters without costly guidance packages and warheads. A still cheaper, though more precarious, Soviet response would be to place a large number of true and fake ICBMs above ground, and to announce a launch-on-warning posture, so that we could not threaten their unprotected missiles. Such additional ICBMs could be deployed in tight clusters, which would greatly aggravate the absentee problem that afflicts all low-orbit in-

terception schemes. A Soviet attack could then begin
with a large proportion of fakes that have precisely the
same booster flares as real ICBMs. Such fakes could
not be ignored by our boost-phase interception systems.
As the laser fuel, pop-up interceptors, or supply of kill
vehicles became depleted, the Soviet attack would shift
to a growing fraction of true ICBMs. These simple
schemes would give the Soviets as realistic (or unrealistic) a first-strike option as they have today, our sophisticated space-based global missile defense notwith-
standing.

In sum, these threatening countermeasures are indeed immensely dangerous to U.S. security. Were the
United States to begin deployment of a new, ultra-
sophisticated BMD system of unknown reliability, the
Soviets could counter by exposing America to a growing force of off-the-shelf weapons whose effectiveness
would not be in doubt, but whose actual numerical
strength and disposition would be secret. In addition,
the Soviets would still be free to invest in new strategic
systems designed to evade space-based BMD, such as
submarine-launched cruise missiles.

ACTIVE COUNTERMEASURES. Active countermeasures are especially effective against space-based
battle stations. Such stations are intrinsically fragile
and vulnerable to the burgeoning armory of anti-satellite weapons. Battle stations will spend months on or
close to known orbits, which makes them very easy to
target compared with boosters, which fly along partially unknown paths for several minutes or less.

Few targets are more attractive than a 10-meter mirror that must retain its shape and reflectivity to a high
degree of perfection if it is to perform its task. It would

be ruined if it were to run into anything placed into orbit by a foe; even a fine cloud of dust would pit the mirror's surface and greatly degrade its ability to focus the beam. One could not protect the mirror with a shield, because it would provide little shelter. If an adversary places a satellite into the same orbit as the mirror, but circling the earth in the *opposite* direction, the relative velocity between the BMD mirror and the adversary's satellite is 16 km per second, which is about eight times faster than an armor-piercing antitank projectile. Were that "anti-BMD" satellite to release a swarm of one-gram steel pellets into the path of the battle station hurtling toward it, these pellets would demolish a two-centimeter-thick aluminium shield covering the mirror. One might try to have the mirror unassembled or folded up if there were no alert. But it is not easy to design a 10-meter mirror that can be pointed with precision better than one part per million toward a target, that must attain a shape accurate to better than a micron, and that can be unfurled as quickly as an umbrella.

The BMD scheme with excimer lasers based on the ground and mirrors in geostationary and low orbits deserves additional comment. The system can be put out of commission by damaging the lasers, or placing light-absorbing material into the atmosphere above the lasers, or both. An attack by submarine-based, salvage-fused missiles on depressed trajectories would be ideal for this purpose. If such missiles struck their targets, the lasers would be demolished. If they did not hit their targets, they would still throw enough dust up to prevent the transmission of the laser beams to the mirrors in space.

Should the Soviet Union also decide to mount a

space-based missile defense, American BMD battle stations would become vulnerable to theirs. Any station that can effectively damage boosters at a range of thousands of kilometers in a minute or less can surely play havoc with a station that is in view for hours on end, and that is likely to be much closer.

There is no need for clever schemes that surgically attack the delicate components of a battle station, however, since the station could be put out of commission by cruder methods. As we have seen, anything released from a counter-rotating "anti-BMD" satellite is totally devastating: to cite one other example, a one-ounce steel pellet moving at 16 km per second would penetrate 15 centimeters of steel. It is not possible to protect a BMD battle station against such a simple and relatively cheap mode of attack.[9]

A most efficient means for attacking a large number of space platforms simultaneously is provided by the *space mine,* a satellite parked in the vicinity of the battle station on the same orbit, which can be detonated at will by remote control just as the ICBM attack gets under way. The space mine can be salvage-fused; as a result, if the owner of the BMD station tampers with it in any way, it explodes and devastates the station.

At first sight, it is natural to discount the space mine as an active countermeasure because the attempt to place a space mine near an opponent's battle station could provoke conflict in peacetime. But that is just the point. The erection of a total BMD system is only superficially a peacetime activity; unless there is an unprecedented level of trust between the superpowers, a missile defense is likely to be perceived as a mortal threat. One cannot expect adherence to the space-age equivalent of the rules of medieval jousting.

Indeed, it would be reckless to attempt the construction of a total BMD system unless one expects to dominate space completely. One should be able to destroy the opponent's satellites at will, prevent their replacement, and deny the opponent the opportunity to place threatening ASAT devices—such as space mines—anywhere within range of one's own BMD battle stations. But technological superiority cannot be relied on for such dominance. A laser battle station that can destroy boosters thousands of kilometers away demands a far higher level of sophistication than a space mine or a pellet swarm that can ruin it at any moment. A bit of history is worth recalling: during World War II, determined Russian infantrymen demolished large numbers of the best tanks then available with Molotov cocktails.

In short, the construction of a total BMD system could in itself lead to open conflict where otherwise there would have been none. The magnitude of that risk would *increase* with the opponent's perception of the effectiveness of one's own BMD systems.

PASSIVE COUNTERMEASURES. We have already mentioned the most important passive countermeasure against boost-phase interception: a booster that burns out quickly inside the atmosphere. Such boosters are immune to X-ray lasers and particle beam weapons. In principle, those directed energy weapons could still be used in an attack after boost phase, but that would be so difficult that it has not been proposed. The post-boost bus that slowly dispenses warheads and decoys could be replaced by a device that would suddenly deploy the decoys and the MIRVs, and this could be done without any loss of accuracy. City-destroying reentry vehicles need no electronics and would be vastly tougher than boosters.

Ordinary laser beams can penetrate into the atmosphere, but shortening boost phase dramatically lessens the time available for interception, a period already too brief for today's boosters.

Other passive boost-phase countermeasures fall into two categories: those that hinder targeting of the booster, and those that seek to protect the booster.

Highly accurate targeting of the booster is possible only if one knows roughly where it is—if the target has been "acquired." The obvious advantage of boost-phase interception is that target acquisition is facilitated by the strong infrared signal emitted by the flare from the missile's engines. But the flare is not the target. The actual target—the booster—is several meters above the top of the flame, and the BMD target-acquisition device would in most schemes have to compute the location of the aim point from the infrared signal. To this end, it will match the infared signal with models of the signal shape and its spatial relation to the booster that have been stored in its computer memory. The aim point determined in this way must drift by no more than a fraction of a meter if the BMD weapon is a laser beam, since those beams must dwell on the *same* target spot for some seconds at a minimum or they will not cause sufficient damage. During that time the booster will have moved tens of miles.

Disguising the target spot is not difficult. One could add "pollutants" to the propellant that burn especially brightly, ejected by various booster nozzles at different times. In contrast to a conventional booster, this one would emit a flame that is both asymmetrical and varied sporadically. Such variations in the infrared signal could not be predicted by the attacker. Under these conditions even a very sophisticated computer code would be hard put to maintain the "gun sight" on one fixed spot on the booster.

So-called skirts are also devices that could deny the defender an accurate sight of the flames. These skirts are hollow cylinders lowered from the booster over the upper portion of the booster flame. They could hide differing fractions of the flame on different missiles and could even move up and down during boost phase. Once again, this would make it very difficult for the BMD target computer to know how far above the flame the real booster is.

Target acquisition can also be impeded by creating a large infrared background against which it is far more difficult to find the booster flares. This can be done by the attacker if he explodes nuclear weapons in the upper atmosphere just before firing his ICBMs.

These countermeasures against target acquisition and accurate aiming are effective against all devices that exploit the infrared signal, lasers as well as kill vehicles. The booster itself can also be protected against damage from laser beams in a variety of ways, though these countermeasures will not be effective against kill vehicles. The booster can be coated with a highly reflecting material, kept clean by a foil overlay during the early stages of boost. It can be spun so the beam does not dwell on the same spot. The booster could also be equipped with heat sensors and a hydraulic system that would bring a coolant to those portions of the skin that are being bathed in a laser beam. One could even equip the booster with a "band-aid," a relatively short cylinder specifically designed to absorb heat that can be moved along the booster at the command of heat sensors to protect the portion under attack. A layer of carbon one centimeter thick would suffice to absorb 200 Megajoules per square meter of heat energy.

There can be little doubt that the boost phase of a strategic ballistic missile attack is the pivotal few minutes for a missile defense. It is in these few minutes (or quite possibly just one minute) that the numerical size of the threat is lowest, and it is during this brief time that the attacking weapons are most vulnerable. The visibility of the booster flame, the relative fragility of the booster, the U.S. military's knowledge of Soviet ICBM silos—all of these factors would seem to present a defender with his best opportunity to knock out the attacker's missile force.

It is equally clear, however, that boost-phase interception is extraordinarily difficult, and perhaps impossible. The curvature of the earth, the shortness of time, the absorption of some kinds of radiation by the atmosphere, and the cost and sheer complexity of a boost-phase defense are daunting enough. The array of simple, effective countermeasures the Soviets could employ, moreover, decisively militates against an effective ballistic missile defense. For without a nearly leakproof boost-phase defense, a multilayered total BMD system is doomed to failure.

6:

MIDCOURSE INTERCEPTION
AND TERMINAL DEFENSE

The midcourse phase of ballistic missile flight begins at the end of the post-boost phase, when the last stage of the booster rocket has completed its task and the MIRV bus has released the warheads along their different paths. The terminal phase of flight starts at the upper reaches of the atmosphere at an altitude of about 100 km, where atmospheric drag first starts to influence the trajectories of the "threat cloud."

The problem of midcourse interception, similar to that of boost phase, is that important components of the BMD must be deployed in space on orbiting platforms or on pop-up systems launched at the moment of attack. In two respects, however, the midcourse problem is very different from boost-phase defense. On the one hand, the defender is assisted by the greater time available for interception, some twenty minutes for ICBMs and less than half that for SLBMs on minimum-energy trajectories. On the other hand, the defender's job is made immensely more difficult by the numerical size of the threat cloud. The proliferation of decoys and other penetration aids following boost phase may confront the defense with hundreds of thousands of objects to be tracked and intercepted. There is no serious obstacle to increasing this number to 1,000,000 or more, although the attacker must pay a weight penalty to do it. To be conservative, we assume the smaller figures.

In the vacuum of space, objects follow identical ballistic trajectories irrespective of their mass and drag characteristics, and this makes discrimination between warheads on reentry vehicles and decoys difficult. The attacker can make discrimination impossible, which would force the defense to intercept every object. The major obstacle to a successful midcourse defense, then, is that sensing and battle-management capabilities are likely to be overwhelmed, particularly if the ICBM attack was not effectively thinned out during its boost phase.

SENSORS AND BATTLE MANAGEMENT

Target acquisition and tracking are much more difficult in midcourse than in boost phase because the objects are far cooler and more numerous. Target acquisition is typically accomplished by "passive" sensing, the detection of visible or infrared light emitted by the target or light from the earth and sun reflected from the target. This sensing requires optical techniques using mirror telescopes fitted with special detectors whose electrical signals are passed on to computers for processing and use by the battle-management system.

Discrimination and tracking may be carried out passively or actively. Active detection and tracking uses light (ladar) or microwaves (radar) to illuminate the target, then processes the reflected signals. By measuring the round-trip signal time, the range to a target can be determined to great accuracy, and from successive range measurements very accurate velocities may be derived. For example, a large ground-based radar can determine both the distance of an object to within about 70 cm from more than 1,600 km away, and its velocity to within 30 cm per second at a speed of more than 6,000 meters per second.

Passive sensing and analysis of light from the target in both the visible and infrared range can be used to determine the temperature and other features of the target. Segmented detectors, comprised of many separate detector elements, are becoming available that can provide thousands to perhaps a million or more picture elements at one time from an optical telescope. They provide a television-like image that helps in target identification and discrimination.

Ladar makes use of very powerful laser light sources. In combination with large, diffraction-limited optics and segmented detectors, and in the absence of countermeasures, ladar can in principle make swift and precise calculations of position and velocity, and can provide information helpful to target discrimination.*

Passive methods may also be used to determine the position and velocity of a target, provided the sensor platform is moving and there is accurate knowledge of its position. This is a space version of triangulation, well known to surveyors, where the known motion of the sensor platform provides the baseline. Because di-

---

*It is also possible, in principle, to probe the target with a burst of X rays from a great distance and discriminate through analysis of the induced X-ray fluorescence. This might also be done by detecting neutrons and gamma rays from fission induced in nuclear warheads by particle beam weapons.

rect range information is lacking, the target track must be established by a computer that makes a mathematical fit of a sequence of angular position measurements to an assumed ballistic orbit. Typically, a hundred seconds of tracking are required, as contrasted with the five or ten needed with an active system. Passive tracking is subject to very effective countermeasures, however, which are discussed below.

There are a number of basing schemes for deployment of the sensors and their ancillary equipment. One possibility is orbiting stations, but these face the problem of extreme vulnerability discussed earlier in connection with boost-phase BMD. Sensor systems can also be popped up, either in a high arc, where they would have a "loiter time" of perhaps ten minutes, or into orbit. Some sensor systems can be carried by high-altitude aircraft. In the absence of countermeasures, airborne optical systems (long-wavelength infrared sensors with laser ranging) can carry out acquisition, discrimination, tracking, and some weapon-firing functions. In contrast to a pop-up system, aircraft can "loiter" for ten hours or more.

All of the components of a midcourse defense must be knit together, as in boost-phase and terminal defense, by a very sophisticated battle-management system comprised of computers and high-speed data links that coordinate the activities of the defensive system. Where the computers would be placed is still an open question. Most might be based in space. Alternatively, the computing could be ground-based, though some information preprocessing on the sensor platforms would probably precede data transmission to the ground, where more powerful computers could be situated. In the latter case, a great deal of information would then have to be retransmitted to whatever space sensors or weapons required it.

WEAPONS

There are as yet no weapons at such a state of development that they could be confidently incorporated in a midcourse missile defense system. The Department of Defense is proceeding with the development of a number of technologies from which it hopes that at least one successful weapon will emerge. The main candidate technologies are lasers, including nuclear-pumped X-ray lasers; charged and neutral particle beams; and projectiles, which may be either self-propelled (rockets) or fired from hypervelocity "rail guns."

Lasers and particle beams are unlikely to fulfill the requirements for midcourse defense, however, for many of same reasons that make them inadequate for boost-phase interception. In addition to those limitations and vulnerabilities, directed energy weapons face another hurdle in midcourse. Targets are many times more numerous and tougher than in boost phase, so the number of directed energy weapons would have to multiply accordingly. That is extraordinarily costly. Because the drawbacks to these weapons appear to be decisive, the remainder of the analysis of midcourse BMD, including countermeasures, will be devoted to the more "promising" technologies of projectiles.

Midcourse interception requires that each reentry vehicle be attacked individually. One might expect that material or charged particles put in space might form a broad shield by destroying objects in a large volume of space, but this is not practical. To put pellets into orbit to form such a shield would require some 50 trillion objects, each weighing less than one ounce but together weighing about a billion tons. For somewhat similar reasons it is not feasible to fill the Van Allen belts with a level of electrons that would be lethal to reentry vehicles. Barrage attack with a nonorbiting pellet screen, although requiring a smaller number of pellets than in the orbiting concept, is unworkable because the objects cannot linger long enough in space to be useful.

Nuclear explosions are also unsuitable for destroying a threat cloud that fills a large volume, although they would seem like an obvious candidate for this task. A nuclear explosion in space could destroy reentry vehicles through radiation damage, thermal energy deposition, X-ray-induced blowoff and impulse, or electromagnetic pulse (EMP) effects that overload components and cause failure of electronic circuits. However, the maximum kill distance is only a few kilometers. To destroy all reentry vehicles over one-fifth of the earth would require about 4 million megatons of nuclear explosive, a totally impractical proposition. While midcourse nuclear explosions would sweep away decoys at much greater distances than they would destroy reentry vehicles—perhaps up to 100 km—and thus reduce the load on sensor and battle-management systems, collateral effects from the detonations would seriously interfere with the functioning of the defense.

One consequence of nuclear explosions above most of the atmosphere might prove useful for both the defense and the offense. This effect, called atmospheric heave, is a consequence of the heating of the upper atmosphere below a nuclear burst by the copious X rays from the burst. The heated air expands upward over a region perhaps 1,000 kilometers square and can produce significant air at altitudes well above 100 km where air density is normally insignificant. Megaton or tens-of-megaton bursts are probably required to produce a usable effect even when the burst is tailored to optimize the X-ray energy distributions, and some focusing of the blast is implemented. Atmospheric heave may allow some degree of target discrimination, especially against large, light balloon decoys by retarding their flight. It is possible that the drag exerted on such decoys at altitudes as great as hundreds of kilometers by the displaced air could lead to a discernible loss in velocity.

Of course, one would have to track each of the balloons in order to establish that it had slowed down. An obvious countermeasure is to tether the decoys to the more massive reentry vehicles. In view of the great difficulty, if not the impossibility, the defense will face in tracking all the objects in the threat cloud, and the very serious problems for the defense caused by the infrared and radar disturbances from the heaved air, lofting a portion of the atmosphere upward may prove an ineffective technique for target discrimination.

Hit-to-kill projectiles can intercept missiles or reentry vehicles provided that they can be deployed and directed promptly in adequate numbers and with sufficient accuracy. The velocities involved in intercepting a target vehicle moving at about 8 km per second are enough to destroy anything by the collision alone without the need for explosives. Projectiles might be self-propelled (for example, with small chemical rockets), or fired by electromagnetic rail guns, and could be based in space or popped up in clusters on large rockets.

The U.S. Army has attempted to develop a homing vehicle for midcourse interception as part of the Homing Overlay project. Three early tests of this system, which uses ground-based radar and airborne infrared sensors, were unsuccessful, but on June 10, 1984, a test using a homing vehicle augmented by a five-meter-diameter steel umbrella destroyed a dummy warhead over the Pacific. This technology has also been exploited by the Air Force for its anti-satellite Miniature Homing Vehicle (MHV), scheduled to be tested in space within a year or so. The MHV homes in on its target using an infrared sensor, and an on-board computer that directs the firing of over fifty small equatorial rockets for guidance. Its homing ability is based on recent major advances in semiconductor integrated circuits.

Homing devices can be autonomous or directed. In autonomous operation a cloud of homing vehicles is launched toward a set of targets, but without specific target assignments. The homing vehicles then "acquire" targets independently, and more than one interceptor may home on the same target with other targets spared. Directed homing vehicles are given specific target assignments by the battle-management system based on information provided by the acquisition and tracking instruments. The battle-management system would almost certainly have to track all the homing vehicles, as well as all objects in the threat cloud, adding substantially to the risk of system overload.

Because of the expected leakage, autonomous homing is inefficient. If 10,000 autonomous homing vehicles are directed at 10,000 reentry vehicle targets, the attack will average 63 percent kill, and 3,700 reentry vehicles will survive. Nearly 70,000 autonomous homing vehicles are needed to reduce the number of surviving reentry vehicles to ten, or a 99.9 percent kill. Similarly, if the threat cloud contains 100,000 objects, then 700,000 vehicles must be sent against them to achieve a 99.9 percent kill. This illustrates the advantage the offense enjoys by using large numbers of objects. Autonomous homing may be required, however, where the tracking and weapons-assignment capacity of the defense is effectively blunted by countermeasures or by overwhelming numbers. A threat cloud comprising hundreds of thousands of objects is not unrealistic, given the poor prospects for boost-phase kill.

An alternative means of delivering homing vehicles is to employ electromagnetic rail guns. Rail guns accelerate the vehicle to extremely high velocity on conducting rails that deliver current to the vehicle. A complete rail gun with aiming and pointing apparatus, communications, self-defense, fuel, and ancillary gear, would be a large and heavy piece of equipment; it would have to be based in space rather than popped up. The goal for rail guns, which are still in the developmental stage, is to achieve vehicle velocities well above 8 km per second and firing rates of around 1 per second. It may be possible, by one or a combination of means, to achieve velocities approaching 40 km per second. Velocities in the range of reentry velocity (about 8 km per second) or greater preclude ground deployment, because the vehicle would be injured or would burn up on its way out of the atmosphere.

COUNTERMEASURES

Nowhere are possible countermeasures to BMD more numerous, and of greater potential effectiveness, than in midcourse. A great variety of decoys and other penetration aids can be deployed. Sensor and battlemanagement systems can be disrupted by masking, signature suppression, and jamming. Some counter-measures and other responses useful in the boost and terminal phases may also be employed during mid-course.

One very effective midcourse countermeasure is the use of decoys. Decoys are devices that simulate the weapon-bearing reentry vehicles. They are typically deployed at the end of boost phase to confuse and over-whelm the BMD battle-management system, and lead to the exhaustion or inefficient use of the defense's weapons. A large number of decoys can be released, perhaps ten or more for each warhead, so the threat cloud in a large attack could easily consist of many hundreds of thousands of objects. The common decoy is a balloon whose material is tailored to give it the infrared and radar signature of a reentry vehicle. Other, lighter objects may be used as well. In the extreme vacuum at midcourse altitudes, the decoys retain their trajectories, just as the heavier vehicles do.

Antisimulation is a more subtle form of decoying. Here both decoys and reentry vehicles may be given varying signatures so that reentry vehicles look like decoys or both look like neither, some of each having properties uncharacteristic of reentry vehicles or nor-mal reentry vehicle decoys. In one form of antisimula-tion a balloon decoy contains a reentry vehicle that is off center, leading a homing vehicle or other weapon to miss its intended target. A balloon can also be tethered a short distance from a reentry vehicle; an interceptor, homing on the composite target, could well pass harm-lessly between the components.

Passive decoys, such as very light corner-reflectors that give especially strong radar or optical reflections, may be used in large quantities. The decoys may be active, with radar transponders. The transponders send back false echos that simulate the normal radar return of objects of a variety of sizes and ranges. These countermeasures confuse and overwhelm the defense's active tracking system. In addition, both decoys and reentry vehicles may be given the capacity to maneuver, frustrating passive tracking schemes that depend on the tracked object remaining on a ballistic trajectory.

It is very useful to the defense to observe the deployment of reentry vehicles and decoys from the MIRV bus at the end of boost phase. With continuous tracking, the later task of discrimination and weapons assignment is then greatly eased. However, it is possible to defeat this technique by erecting a "modesty" shield around the space bus during its unloading phase, or by quick release of warheads and decoys.

Decoys need not be deployed solely at the end of boost phase but can also be released on an arbitrary schedule during midcourse flight. This would add to the burden of both active and passive tracking and would replace the decoys swept away by defensive use of nuclear weapons. Decoy deployment, or other forms of spoofing, could also be triggered by any indication that a reentry vehicle was being fired on. A hit could be simulated, much as World War II submarines would release oil or bubbles when under attack.

Masking, signature suppression, and jamming can be achieved by simple techniques that disrupt the sensor and battle-management system of the defense. The use of chaff—clouds of metallic strands or wire—can saturate defense radars and mask the return of signals from objects of interest. Chaff will travel with the threat cloud until swept out by the atmosphere on reentry.

Infrared reflecting aerosols, which will reflect infrared radiation from the earth, may be ejected from a reentry vehicle or MIRV bus. This reflected energy will mask and obscure infrared target signatures. Another technique is to employ multilayer, aluminized plastic covers over reentry vehicles or for balloon material. This greatly reduces radiated heat and thermal signatures, making temperature measurements difficult or ambiguous. The materials can also be blackened to reduce this optical reflectivity, making the object less visible.

Atmospheric heave induced by precursor bursts preceding an attack launch could be a countermeasure both for defensive X-ray lasers and neutral particle beams, especially if the defense employed low-energy particle beams. Bursts above 100 km, with an X-ray energy spectrum giving rapid atmospheric absorption, might raise the atmospheric density at altitudes from 120 to 200 km enough to provide satisfactory shielding where otherwise the launch vehicles and buses would be vulnerable to attack. This prospective countermeasure warrants further study, but its effectiveness is not yet established.

Finally, special measures can be adopted to increase the resistance of reentry vehicles to midcourse attack. While little can be done to harden a vehicle to withstand the impact of a homing vehicle, resistance to laser beams can be substantially improved. Reflecting materials will decrease energy absorption, and ablative technology—such as that used to resist the heat of reentry—can increase hardness against energy deposition weapons. Rotation of the target can reduce local heating from continuous wave laser weapons so as to increase the already long dwell times that will be required if these devices are ever perfected.

TERMINAL DEFENSE

Increasing atmospheric drag begins to sweep out the lighter objects in the threat cloud at altitudes of around 60 km, and a plasma sheath starts to form around the heavier objects. This sheath, and a fiery tail composed of ionized air along with particles of ablative material from the nose cone, is luminous, and the vehicles begin to scintillate. These characteristics of reentry and the terminal phase make discrimination of warheads from decoys much easier. The deceleration can be as much as one hundred times the acceleration of gravity. Reentry typically lasts about one minute. The narrow, low-drag reentry vehicles typical of those in the U.S. inventory reach the ground with a velocity of about 3 km per second at an angle with the horizontal of 20 degrees.

The terminal layer of a total BMD must be an area defense capable of protecting soft targets, particularly cities and other populated areas. Its task is thus very different, and much more difficult, than a hard-point defense of hardened military targets such as missile silos.

The emphasis of previous American BMD programs, including the Safeguard ABM briefly deployed in the 1970s, has been on hard-point defense, for which the technological requirements are fairly well understood. Two features make the job of the hard-point defense easier. First, hardened targets must be attacked by groundburst or low airburst weapons of high accuracy. This allows the defender to intercept at close range (even within a fraction of a kilometer from the target), leaving more time for tracking and discrimination. Second, a high leakage rate may be acceptable in defending military targets. For example, in a defense of land-based missile silos, a target survival rate of 10 to 15 percent would still preserve a devastating retaliatory capability, even omitting the remaining elements of the bomber force and the submarines at sea. The prospect of that surviving ICBM force would suffice to deter a strike by the adversary. This fact makes possible a preferential defense of hard targets in which some are defended and others not.[10]

In contrast, the defense of populations against nuclear attack requires that all targets (in effect, the whole urban territory of the United States) be defended at long range, and that leakage be reduced to near zero. These requirements give the attacker advantages and options that pose intractable problems for terminal defenses. Much higher bursts and lower accuracies will produce a successful attack. Indeed, terminal defenses could invite the introduction of weapons of greater yield than are now employed, which could be detonated at very high altitude. As an extreme example, a 50-megaton weapon—a yield the Soviets once tested but did not deploy—exploded at an altitude of 30 km will set fires and do major damage from blast over more than 1,600 square kilometers.

Tracking problems would be complicated not only by the need to commit interceptors very early, but because the trajectories of reentry vehicles descending toward cities would not converge on well-defined aim points as in the case of warheads aimed at hard targets. Reentry vehicles that can maneuver compound the problem: their midcourse trajectories could imply aim points up to 100 km from the desired targets. Using stubby winglets or a canted nose, a warhead could maneuver to its target during reentry at hypersonic velocities, seriously stressing the defense. There are few ways to cope with such vehicles. The defense could attempt to develop a much higher velocity homing vehicle than now seems practical or move to the unpalatable use of 1-to-2-kiloton nuclear interception weapons with all the difficulties this poses for the defense.

Finally, the defense must face the near-certain threat of attacks directed at the extensive, and very soft, radars and battle-management systems that would be required to control the defenses. As in the case of midcourse defense, these would be relatively easy to destroy. Because of the stringent leakage criterion, the loss of even a very small portion of the tracking and command system would make the defense ineffective

This discussion of post-boost defense underscores the reasons why the boost phase is so crucial to a total defense system. The proliferation of warheads and decoys in midcourse and the insoluble problems of protecting cities in the terminal phase of a strategic attack conspire to place the burden of BMD schemes on boost-phase interception. And that is a burden that the current schemes for ballistic missile defense cannot bear.

7:

SYSTEMIC PROBLEMS AND NET ASSESSMENT

There are systemic weaknesses in the Star Wars concept that transcend the shortcomings of individual weapons and the deadliness of countermeasures—problems that affect all phases of the defense. Any scheme for a total missile defense must overcome two generic problems. The first is the vulnerability of the defense to attacks—including nuclear attacks—on its ground- and space-based components. The second is that the system can never be tested under conditions that are remotely realistic, and therefore one will never know with confidence that it would work if called upon. This chapter examines these generic problems and provides our net assessment of the prospects for a total missile defense.

SYSTEMIC PROBLEMS

DEFENSE SUPPRESSION. One of the most effective tactics that can be employed against a ballistic missile defense is to attack the ground- and space-based systems on which it depends. Some of these assets are surprisingly vulnerable. Nuclear explosions in space, as we have already mentioned, can blind infrared sensors and black out radars. Detonated ahead of the flight of reentry vehicles, at altitudes of from 60 to 80 km, a single "precursor" burst will ionize a region of space some tens of kilometers across, hiding the vehicles for several minutes. Anti-radiation homing vehicles may be used to destroy radars in space and on the ground. Space mines or inert objects, including sand, may be used against fragile space-based lasers and mirrors. A variety of measures can be taken to jam, spoof, and confuse the data-transfer links of the battle-management system.

Should the X-ray laser prove to be workable, it could be effective in the service of the attacker even though it would not be useful in defense. The attacker could fire X-ray lasers at high altitudes and use them to blind the sensors or otherwise damage the opponent's space-based BMD system.

Because of the immense damage that they would do to their targets, attacks from submarine-launched ballistic missiles and cruise missile attacks can be a decisive factor in defense suppression. Submarine-launched missiles have short flight times, giving as little as three to five minutes warning for near-coastal targets. They have unpredictable launch points, which can make viewing angles poor for the defense. Moreover, SLBMs can be launched on depressed trajectories, low enough to allow the missiles to evade most defenses. Cruise missiles are low-flying and nearly invisible to optical and radar trackers. The BMD system cannot defend itself against such attacks. In the future, if an extensive missile defense moves toward deployment, increasing attention would have to be paid to submarine missile attacks. Some improvements in sea-launched ballistic missile defense can be expected, but it is difficult to see what can be done to mitigate the cruise missile threat.

Targets of cruise or sea-launched missiles would include ground facilities for battle management, rockets and basing facilities associated with pop-up sensors and weaponry, and communications and control stations. Well-executed strikes of this sort, in advance of the main offensive missile launch, would in all likelihood disable the entire defense structure.

SOFTWARE AND ALGORITHMS. The battle-management systems of a total BMD must deal with hundreds of thousands of objects. This requires computers with the capacity to carry out many hundreds of millions, if not billions, of arithmetic operations per second. Advances in computer technology suggest that the hardware to accomplish this monumental task may become available in the future. There are, however, several challenges whose solutions are doubtful. One is the problem of designing and writing the programs (software) required to guide the computers. Experience with earlier defense-system software (as well as non-defense examples) suggests that it will be exceedingly difficult, if not impossible, to construct software that could operate properly in the environment of a nuclear attack. As Dr. DeLauer stated to the House Armed Services Committee, "the information processing capability to associate outputs from multiple sensors, perform discrimination and 'birth-to-death' tracking plus kill assessment is expected to stress software development technology." Such software could never be fully tested.

A related problem is that of developing algorithms for tracking and especially for discrimination and weapons assignment. Algorithms are the rules or criteria by which the sensor data on range, velocity, maneuvering, and other target properties are assessed, weapon commitments made, damage evaluated, and weapons reassigned and committed. There would be one or more algorithms, for example, to decide which objects were decoys and which were lethal objects. Indeed, in fast-response defense systems, the computer code could well embody essential elements of U.S. national policy for initiating attack.

The algorithms must be prepared long in advance of conflict and embedded in software and, to some extent, hardware. They are critical to the performance of the defense. Not only must these algorithms cope with the opponent's countermeasures, whose nature and effectiveness could only be guessed at in advance, but they must be free of internal flaws. As with the software, it is virtually impossible to be confident that a fatal flaw is not embedded somewhere in these criteria. An example of such a flaw is the guidance of far too many weapons toward unusual or unexpected decoys and away from warheads. The inability to test a ballistic missile defense system fully before it is used makes the prospect of errors most unsettling. And it is with respect to the battle-management system—the hardware, software, and the algorithms—that this deficiency can have some of its gravest consequences.

CONFIDENCE. Suppose for a moment that a total missile defense system without obvious flaws had been developed and deployed. This defense, in a time of confrontation and nuclear attack, would represent the only prospect of avoiding overwhelming ruin. Could there be enough confidence in this defense that the United States could safely reduce its nuclear forces unilaterally? Or could the United States, during a crisis, ignore Soviet nuclear threats with impunity? The confidence that is needed is not merely that each component of the myriad array of parts—the sensors, the weapons, the computers—would, individually, perform as expected. More important is the need for confidence that the entire assembly would operate as a harmonious machine and capably blunt the attack. Consider the nature of the defensive system: an enormous and complex assemblage; novel in design and pushing the limits of technology; intended to provide a defense against a threat that will be fully known only when the attack comes; and forced to meet an uncommonly high standard of performance. And, remarkably enough, it cannot ever have been adequately tested.

No amount of testing under simulated battle conditions could confidently explore the response of a complex defensive system to an actual nuclear attack. In part, this is because the nature of the attack and the attacker's countermeasures, as well as their effectiveness, cannot be known in advance. It is also because one cannot simulate the stress and the demands on the system of the circumstances of war.

The matter of testing is crucial. The performance of complex devices can rarely be ensured before they meet realistic conditions, even when their tasks are well defined. Complex designs breed complex problems. This is also the case with computer software. All large programs contain bugs or hidden flaws, and while their number dwindles over time as the programs are used, no one can ever be certain that the bugs are gone, and new circumstances can bring new flaws to light. Ironically, even if an apparently effective defense could be prepared, it is highly unlikely that much trust would be placed in its working properly when needed.

Without confidence in the defense, the most important of the president's goals in pursuing space defense recedes and becomes unattainable. Nuclear weapons cannot be made "impotent and obsolete" until, and unless, we have a defense we can trust. Without confidence in the defense there can be no relief from the threat posed by offensive missiles and no transition to a defense-based world.

NET ASSESSMENT OF STAR WARS TECHNOLOGY

BASING. The requirement that a total BMD operate largely in space creates an insoluble basing dilemma. On the one hand, orbiting stations, whether for weapons, sensors, or mirrors, are inherently fragile and vulnerable to attack by space mines and other ASAT techniques. This vulnerability would make them provocative targets during a developing crisis and thus might actually help precipitate the outbreak of conflict. On the other hand, the alternatives to orbital basing—airborne, ground-based, or pop-up systems—are, in important respects, inferior in their ability to perform BMD functions in boost phase and midcourse. There has been no satisfactory scheme put forward for using the X-ray laser, the only directed energy weapon that could in theory be popped up as a component of a BMD system. X-rays cannot penetrate the atmosphere and it is perfectly practical to reduce boost phase so burnout occurs inside the atmosphere. Furthermore, the impact of the X-ray beam is too weak to damage warheads following boost phase. The ground-based excimer laser, another prominent boost-phase candidate, relies on orbiting mirrors that would be extremely vulnerable.

SENSORS AND BATTLE MANAGEMENT. Both active and passive tracking, discrimination systems, and the associated battle-management facilities can be seriously compromised both by countermeasures and by the large number of nearly indistinguishable objects comprising the threat cloud. These problems are likely to be insuperable in midcourse, and, as a result, a BMD system would have to forgo any attempt at tracking each individual object. Individual weapons assignments are thus impossible. The only alternative is to allow the interceptors to home at random on all the objects in the threat cloud. But this is highly inefficient, requiring on the order of one million homing vehicles or more for the expected Soviet threat.

WEAPONS. Particle beam weapons are unpromising for boost-phase interception; the prospects of developing them to a satisfactory level of performance seem dim at best, although if unopposed in space they could be excellent ASATs. Laser prospects are far from bright. The improvements that are required are of such magnitude that important technical breakthroughs appear to be needed. All of the particle beam weapons and most of the lasers must be based in space, with all the vulnerability that implies. This vulnerability was emphasized by the Fletcher panel: *"Survivability of the system components is a critical issue whose resolution requires a combination of technologies and tactics that remain to be worked out"* [emphasis in original].

The free electron laser is, at this time, not much more than a laboratory curiosity, and no one can be sure what its future will be. But any ground-based laser system must use a large number of mirrors in space, and those mirrors would be extremely vulnerable. In any case, potential countermeasures—such as atmospheric nuclear bursts in the beam path or attacks on the mirrors—threaten all such directed energy weapons.

At the present time, self-propelled homing weapons are the most fully developed of potential BMD weapons. The anti-satellite Miniature Homing Vehicle has been successfully demonstrated in the more difficult task of intercepting a reentry vehicle; as an air-launched MHV, it is approaching deployable status. Technical improvements in speed, guidance accuracy, and maneuverability appear feasible. Yet it is still far from clear that these homing vehicles can become usable weapons for missile defense. And having a satisfactory weapon is still a long way from having a satisfactory defense.

Our analysis makes clear that total ballistic missile defense—the protection of American society against the full weight of a Soviet nuclear attack—is unattainable if the Soviet Union exploits the many vulnerabilities intrinsic to all the schemes that have been proposed thus far. In none of the three phases of attack can one expect a success rate that would reduce the number of warheads arriving on U.S. territory sufficiently to prevent unprecedented death and destruction. Instead, each phase presents intractable problems, and the resulting failure of the system compounds from one phase to the next.

A highly efficient boost-phase interception is a

prerequisite of total BMD, but is doomed by the inherent limitations of the weapons, insoluble basing dilemmas, and an array of offensive countermeasures. As a result, the failure of midcourse systems is preordained. Midcourse BMD is plagued not so much by the laws of physics and geometry as by the sheer unmanageability of its task in the absence of a ruthless thinning out of the attack in boost phase.

Terminal phase BMD remains fundamentally unsuitable for area defense of population centers as opposed to hard-point targets. There seems to be no way of defending soft targets on a continent-wide basis against the broad variety of attacks that could be tailored to circumvent and overwhelm terminal defenses.

8:

POLITICAL AND STRATEGIC IMPLICATIONS

The political and strategic dangers raised by the Star Wars initiative are at least as important as its technical flaws. These dangers would weigh heavily against development of ballistic missile defenses even if their technical prospects were much brighter than they are. A U.S. commitment to BMD would precipitate Soviet responses and a chain of actions and reactions that would radically change the strategic environment to the detriment of both countries' security. The first adverse consequence would be the demise of the ABM Treaty, and with it the negotiated constraints on offensive nuclear forces. The offensive arms race would then accelerate, the entire arms control process would be compromised, the NATO alliance strained, and the nuclear peace made more precarious.

The technical and political issues are not completely unconnected. If it were possible to put in place overnight a fully effective, invulnerable defense against nuclear weapons, there could hardly be serious objections to doing so. As the preceding analysis has shown, however, such a system cannot be built now or, in all likelihood, ever. In the real world, BMD systems will be imperfect. Even under very optimistic assumptions about their ultimate performance, the process of improvement would be incremental and prolonged. During this extended and highly unstable transition period, the strategic and political implications of BMD become critical.

While the alleged benefits of BMD are distant and hypothetical, the dangers are near-term and predictable. The adverse consequences of a commitment to BMD would be felt long before deployment. These consequences would follow the familiar action-reaction syndrome, driven by the highly threatening nature of BMD and the worst-case assumptions that would guide nuclear planning amid large uncertainties about the effectiveness of BMD systems and ambiguities about the intentions behind them. Accordingly, the dangers posed by a U.S. policy of ballistic missile defense would be virtually independent of the level of performance that BMD systems might, decades in the future, finally achieve.

THE SOVIET RESPONSE TO BMD AND PROSPECTS FOR ARMS CONTROL

Thirty years of cold war have created a barrier of mistrust that dominates the superpowers' perceptions of each other. Each side appears to take for granted the aggressive intentions of the other, even when such an interpretation is unwarranted by the facts As a result, the Star Wars initiative, which President Reagan may believe is a *defensive* program, has been repeatedly described as *offensive* by the Soviets. It is apparently seen as part of an American effort to acquire a first-strike capability—the ability to launch a devastating attack against Soviet strategic forces and to defend effectively against a poorly coordinated and depleted Soviet retaliatory strike. When BMD is coupled with the on-going American buildup of counterforce weapons, such as the MX and Trident II, and America's adoption of a warfighting doctrine, the Soviet Union's conviction of U.S. first-strike planning will grow firmer. Indeed, the president himself acknowledged in his speech of March 23, 1983, that ballistic missile defense, "if paired with offensive systems . . . can be viewed as fostering an aggressive policy."

The Soviet Union is no more likely than the United States to accept a position of strategic inferiority. In addition to working on its own BMD, the Soviets should be expected to develop forces that can penetrate or circumvent American defenses. As described in Chapter 5, the Soviets could develop a number of countermeasures: they could reduce the duration of the boost phase of their ICBMs, disguise the booster's flame to make their missiles more difficult to target, or deploy a large number of decoys to confuse and strain the defense. All of these countermeasures are based on existing technology, and many are relatively inexpensive.

The surest way to defeat a BMD is to swamp it. An American BMD would encourage the Soviets to continue to develop large ICBMs, which offer the most efficient means of delivering large numbers of warheads, decoys, and other penetration aids to overwhelm a BMD system. The Scowcroft Commission on U.S. Strategic Forces cited BMD penetration as an important rationale for U.S. deployment of the ten-warhead MX missile:

The possibility of either a sudden breakthrough in ABM technology, a rapid Soviet breakout from the ABM treaty by a quick further deployment of their current ABM systems, or the deployment of air defense systems having some capability against strategic ballistic missiles all point to the need for us to be able to penetrate some level of ABM defense. This dictates continued attention to having sufficient throwweight for adequate numbers of warheads and of decoys and other penetration aids.[11]

The Soviets would arrive at the same conclusion were the United States to proceed with the Strategic Defense Initiative.

Reagan administration officials have sometimes suggested that a U.S.-Soviet BMD competition would play to U.S. technological strengths. Whether or not this is true, it is clear that a BMD-driven offensive arms race would give the Soviet Union important advantages. Due to both its large advantage in missile throwweight and the absence of political constraints comparable with those in the United States, the Soviet Union is much better positioned for a rapid offensive buildup. If the SALT II agreement, which puts a cap on the deployment of offensive arms, becomes a dead letter, the Soviets could quickly and simply double the number of warheads on their existing heavy missiles. The Soviets' SS-18, for example, is limited under SALT II to ten warheads but could accommodate twenty to thirty. The United States does not now have a missile to accommodate such large numbers of warheads.

In addition to offensive efforts to overwhelm U.S. missile defenses, the Soviets can also be expected to invest in delivery systems that would circumvent those defenses. These include cruise missiles and depressed-trajectory ballistic missiles, discussed in Chapter 4, and more unconventional approaches, such as the "pre-delivery" of atomic weapons by emplacing them clandestinely on U.S. territory. These easily attainable delivery schemes would not only foil U.S. missile defenses, but could reduce warning times and make it much more difficult to assess the Soviets' offensive capabilities by satellite surveillance. As a result, arms control would be more difficult to achieve, and stability would be undercut.

In these circumstances, the Reagan administration's suggestion that BMD might improve the prospects for negotiated arms reduction is unrealistic. Even less plausible is the idea that an American BMD could be used as a lever, in Dr. Keyworth's words, to "pressure the Soviets to take our arms reductions proposals more seriously than they do now." The fact is that the administration's own build-down proposal, introduced at the Strategic Arms Reductions Talks in 1983, would be directly undermined by a U.S. BMD initiative. The "build-down idea emphasizes cuts in the heavy, multiple-warhead Soviet ICBMs that threaten American land-based missiles and seeks an overall restructuring of strategic forces away from MIRVed missiles towards smaller, single-warhead ICBMs. As we have seen, however, an American commitment to BMD would provide the Soviets with even greater incentives for holding on to their heavy ICBMs and possibly even to increase their number."[12]

If, as is likely, the Soviets augment their offensive strategic capability in response to American development of a BMD, the construction of a missile defense could actually increase the destruction that the United States would suffer in a nuclear war. One reason for this is Soviet uncertainty about the effectiveness of American defenses. So as not to take any chances, the Soviets are likely to build up their strategic forces far beyond what would be necessary to maintain strategic parity. Comparative military assessments are almost always based on worst-case analysis, because strategic analysts are most sensitive to the capabilities of their adversary and the deficiencies of their own forces. They must base their assessments on uncertain and incomplete data about the performance and reliability of weapons on both sides, but especially those of the adversary. The less that is known about the quality or quantity of the other side's weapons, the greater the tendency to assign high values to them in order to be safe. A U.S. missile defense assessed by American defense planners as 50 percent effective, for example, might elicit a Soviet buildup based on the assumption of 90 percent effectiveness.

In the past, worst-case analysis has led to American predictions of a bomber gap, a missile gap, and an ABM gap, none of which materialized. Some are already predicting a laser gap; the U.S. Air Force, for example, recently announced that the Soviet Union has a ten-year lead in the development of some crucial aspects of laser weapons. Soviet analysts surely have similarly exaggerated notions of American technical progress and the performance of American weapons. In both countries, extreme assessments of threat are encouraged because they provide rationales for expanded defense budgets.

Using worst-case analysis, each side will interpret actual parity in weapons as an imbalance favoring their adversary, driving both to augment and modernize their arsenals. Tensions will then rise as each side interprets an arms buildup as proof of the other's hostile intentions. The current Soviet and American inability to agree about either the conventional or nuclear balance in Europe offers a telling example of just how this dynamic operates.

A BMD competition would create a far tenser situation because it would be interpreted by both superpowers as vitally threatening. Fear of the military or political consequences of strategic vulnerability might lead the nation that perceives itself as disadvantaged to consider waging a war to prevent BMD deployment.

This is not an idle concern. The 1962 Cuban missile crisis, the most serious superpower confrontation to date, was probably touched off by such fears of vulnerability. The most widely accepted interpretation of the Soviets' attempt to put missiles into Cuba is that it was a desperate effort to redress the strategic balance.* If Cuba offers any guide to the future, there will be a real risk of a major crisis between the superpowers during the time both are struggling to perfect and deploy their defensive systems. As progress toward deployment is unlikely to be symmetrical, the disadvantaged side may well feel driven to do something radical to prevent its own vulnerability. Ironically, the nation that deploys missile defense first—regardless of its technical performance—could pay a great price for its efforts without reaping any return.

*In the fall of 1961 the Kennedy administration decided to tell the Soviets that it knew that their first-generation ICBM had proven a failure in the hope of moderating Khrushchev's bellicosity over Berlin. However, it also put the Soviets on notice that the United States, thanks to a satellite reconnaissance, realized the Soviets' vulnerability to a first strike. Soviet deployment of missiles in Cuba may well have been conceived of as a quick fix to compensate for their strategic inferiority.

THE IMPACT OF BMD ON CRISIS STABILITY AND DETERRENCE

The dangers associated with ballistic missile defense will not subside even if the peace is kept throughout the period when defenses are being developed and deployed. Missile defense in place would be profoundly destabilizing: it would increase the risk of nuclear war during U.S.-Soviet confrontations, and reduce the chances of controlling hostilities if war did break out.

A crisis is more likely to lead to war when the military balance is unstable. Once military leaders on one or both sides believe that war is a real possibility and that they can gain an advantage—perhaps a decisive one—by striking first, they are likely to contemplate a preemptive attack. Under such circumstances, even *defensive* measures can make expectations of war self-fulfilling prophecies. Defenses that are perceived as aggressive can provoke a response and aggravate the anxiety that prompted the original defensive action. Escalation can thereby assume a logic and momentum of its own and stampede policymakers into war. This dynamic was a major cause of war in 1914. The mobilization plans of the European powers placed a premium on speed. Hesitation was believed to be fatal. Like runners nervously anticipating the discharge of a starting gun, the military chiefs eyed each other apprehensively lest one of them get a head start. As often happens in real races, the tension led one participant, Russia, to jump the gun, and the others, fearing they would be left behind, followed suit.

Developments during the last decade have created a similar situation of instability between the superpowers. Both have developed the capability to destroy mili-

tary facilities—command centers and missile silos—
and both have embraced nuclear warfighting doctrines.
These doctrines put a premium on land-based missiles
because these weapons can destroy hardened military
targets. Such doctrines also depend on the survival of
C^3I—the facilities for the communication, command,
control, and intelligence gathering necessary to fight a
limited or protracted nuclear war. Land-based missiles
and C^3I facilities are, however, among the most vulnerable of strategic assets. This vulnerability, coupled with
the missiles' indispensable mission in warfighting scenarios, encourages commanders to adopt a "use 'em or
lose 'em" mentality. For only by striking first can these
important assets be exploited fully. A massive and well-
coordinated first strike also holds out the prospect of
preserving some C^3I facilities by reducing the forces the
other side would use to destroy them.

The pressure to preempt in a crisis would be greatly
intensified in the aftermath of BMD deployments for
four reasons. First, such systems would be a highly
vulnerable portion of a nation's strategic arsenal. Second, a defense would be of questionable utility against
a full-scale attack, but may be quite effective against a
retaliatory strike. Third, even if a space-based BMD is
ineffective against enemy ICBM boosters, its lasers
could have the ability to destroy the adversary's communication and early-warning satellites almost instantly. Fourth, the time for human decision making
would be exceedingly short, because boost-phase inter-
ceptions must be initiated within seconds of warning of
an attack; the BMD software package would have to
contain major portions of a nation's strategic war plans.
These factors would combine to increase the pressure
on political leaders to launch a first strike in a serious

crisis. As this reality would be known to both sides, it would generate yet greater pressures to preempt for fear that the adversary was about to do so.

BMD advocates often claim that U.S. defenses would strengthen deterrence, or limit the resulting damage should deterrence fail. Such arguments are attempts to construct rationales for only modestly capable BMD systems. As such, they represent a very large retreat from President Reagan's vision of transcending (not reinforcing) the system of nuclear deterrence by making nuclear weapons "impotent and obsolete." Nevertheless, these justifications for imperfect BMD systems are important to address. As the president's original vision is increasingly understood to be illusory, an American BMD program is likely to be promoted on grounds of deterrence and damage-limitation. Administration officials and supporters have increasingly argued in these terms during the period since President Reagan's speech.[13] In this regard, one must note the close link between these more modest BMD roles and the administration's early emphasis on nuclear warfighting—a link that will not be overlooked by the Soviet Union.

The notion that BMD would strengthen nuclear deterrence rests mainly on the claim that defenses would reduce the vulnerability of U.S. land-based missiles to a preemptive first strike. By protecting America's ability to retaliate, it is argued, BMD would make a Soviet first strike less certain of success, and therefore less likely. This is really an argument for terminal, hard-point defense of U.S. missile silos, not for the layered, area defenses proposed by the president. The administration's initiative is not only vastly more expensive and complex than is necessary for the protection of retaliatory forces, but it is provocative to the Soviet Union in a way that would reduce, not enhance, deterrent stability.

The damage-limitation rationale for BMD is as dubious as the deterrence argument. This has two variants. First, should deterrence fail and a nuclear war start, it is argued that defenses could save lives and reduce the threat of "assured destruction." Second, we are told, this damage-limitation effect would strengthen deterrence by making the threat of nuclear retaliation more credible. BMD advocates who emphasize these points generally subscribe to the theory that credible deterrence requires forces designed for actual warfighting, capable of being used in a selective, flexible manner. In this context, the damage-limitation role of a BMD system is seen as useful not only to limit population fatalities but also to protect nuclear command and control systems.

These arguments are implausible in light of the size and destructive power of superpower nuclear arsenals and the adjustments in targeting and nuclear strategy that BMD deployments would bring about. The overkill capacity of both superpowers is such that only a near-perfect defense could hope to reduce fatalities appreciably in the event of major nuclear exchanges. For example, if the Soviet Union were to target its missile to maximize damage to the U.S. population—a likely response to a serious American attempt to protect cities—it would need only 5 percent of its *current* ballistic missile warheads to kill up to half of the U.S. urban population immediately (see Figure 19). In other words, even a 95 percent effective BMD would leave the United States with the prospect of tens of millions of prompt fatalities in a nuclear war, leaving aside all

Figure 18. *Effect of BMD Leakage on U.S. Urban Fatalities.* Even if an American BMD system were 95 percent effective, the number of Soviet warheads falling on U.S. cities could cause more than 30 million deaths. NOTE: Aimpoints chosen to maximize prompt human fatalities; assumes Soviet ICBM and SLBM warhead total of 7,500, and U.S. urban population of 131 million (1970 census).
SOURCE: Arms Control and Disarmament Agency, *U.S. Urban Population Vulnerability* (1979), cited in Carter and Schwartz, eds., *Ballistic Missile Defense* (Brookings, 1984).

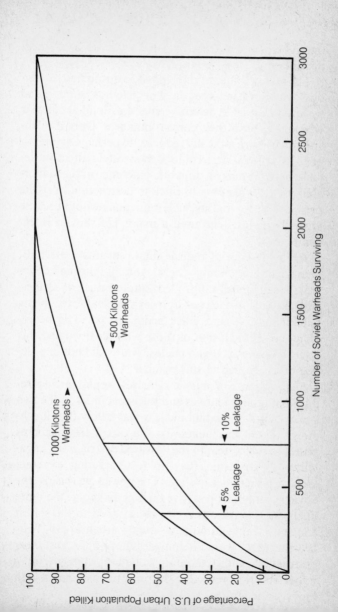

the subsequent deaths from fire, disease, and social disruption.

The vulnerability of the United States to destruction by Soviet nuclear forces, in short, cannot be mitigated by any foreseeable defensive shield as long as nuclear weapons exist in their current numbers. Only if offensive forces were radically reduced, to perhaps one-tenth of their present size, could a moderately effective defense begin to make a dramatic difference in the vulnerability of populations to nuclear destruction. Yet the prospect of negotiating such reductions would become virtually nonexistent amid a major U.S.-Soviet BMD competition.

In the absence of radical cuts in offensive arsenals, damage limitation might be sought only through deliberate strategies of controlled, limited nuclear strikes, with the bulk of each superpower's nuclear forces being held in reserve and cities being spared. The nearly unanimous conclusion of those who have studied this issue, however, is that a nuclear war could not in practice be controlled in this manner.[14]

Deployments of missile defenses would further reduce both the incentives and the capabilities of the two superpowers to contain nuclear war below the threshold of all-out exchanges. To the extent that defenses pose a serious threat to the "assured destruction" capability of either side, they invite retargeting to retain such destructive capacity. The fewer warheads the Soviets can expect to arrive on U.S. territory, the more likely these warheads are to be assigned to the softest and most valuable targets—major urban areas. Warhead accuracy would become less important, and sheer destruction, with maximum collateral damage, more important, thus reversing the priorities associated with limited war strategies.

Far from contributing to a strategy of limited nuclear war, BMD points in the opposite direction—toward massive, indiscriminate exchanges and the erosion of control over strategic forces. Instead of damage limitation, a nuclear war fought under these circumstances could produce higher numbers of fatalities than one fought in the absence of defenses.

THE ABM TREATY

The ballistic missile defense envisaged by the Reagan administration is plainly inconsistent with the 1972 Anti-Ballistic Missile Treaty. As acknowledged in the president's Fiscal Year 1984 Arms Control Impact Statement, the treaty "bans the development, testing, and deployment of all ABM systems and components that are sea-based, air-based, space-based, or mobile land-based." The statement further notes explicitly that the ban on space systems applies to directed energy technologies. Under the interpretation of "development" offered by the United States at the time the treaty was signed, the treaty's prohibitions take effect at the point that ABM systems or components enter the phase of field testing.

The treaty and its 1974 Protocol limit the United States and the Soviet Union each to a single ABM deployment area, including 100 interceptor missiles. Only the Soviet Union currently exercises this deployment option, with the Galosh defense around Moscow.* The United States deactivated its ABM

---

*The Galosh system is a traditional terminal defense of the type the United States pursued in the 1960s and early 1970s. It employs a large, nuclear-armed exoatmospheric interceptor, peripheral radar for target acquisition, and on-site radar for battle management. The system suffers from the inherent limitations that caused the United States to abandon the Sentinel/Safeguard approach to ABM—espe-

installation at Grand Forks, North Dakota, in the mid-
1970s. The treaty permits ABM development and testing subject to a number of serious constraints,
including those on basing noted above. In addition, it
imposes constraints on air defense systems and early
warning radar to limit their possible use in ABM roles.
The purpose of these restrictions is to reinforce the
treaty's effectiveness by preventing either country from
laying the groundwork for a "breakout," or quick deployment of an extensive ABM system.

The ABM Treaty is of great importance in both
practical and symbolic terms. It embodies an implicit
recognition that effective territorial defense against nuclear weapons is not feasible, and that pursuit of such
a defense would be destabilizing and would preclude
limitations on offensive nuclear forces. These premises
are still valid, and the treaty therefore remains firmly
in the mutual interest of the two superpowers. Unilateral abandonment of the treaty by either country would
be tantamount to a rejection of the arms control process per se, and would have highly damaging political
and military consequences for the U.S.-Soviet relationship.

---

cially radar vulnerability and limited target-handling capabilities.
During the past few years the Soviets have been developing the
components of an improved system, designated the ABM-X-3, including two new missiles (one a high-acceleration endoatmospheric
interceptor similar to the U.S. Sprint) and a transportable phased
array radar. The new interceptors may be intended for deployment
in the Galosh system, which has also been upgraded with a large
battle-management radar at Pushkino. Despite these improvements,
the Moscow ABM is not considered by U.S. defense planners to pose
serious obstacles to an American nuclear strike. See especially Sayre
Stevens, "The Soviet BMD Program," in Ashton Carter and David
Schwartz, eds., *Ballistic Missile Defense,* Washington, D.C.: Brookings Institution, 1984.

Although the Strategic Defense Initiative is potentially the most serious threat to the ABM Treaty, it is not the first or only such threat. Rather, developments in both countries already jeopardize the treaty's integrity. Of particular concern are the development of anti-satellite and advanced air defense systems that may have some BMD capability, and recent charges and countercharges of treaty violations. Taken together, these trends suggest that a turning point is approaching: the superpowers must either reaffirm their commitment to the treaty or risk an irreversible decline of confidence in it.

Because of their overlap with missile defense technologies, ASATs could erode the treaty's ban on development and testing of space-based missile defenses. As ASAT programs proceed, the question of whether or not they have some ABM capabilities—and are therefore inconsistent with the treaty—will be increasingly prominent but difficult to resolve.*

The issue of treaty compliance has loomed especially large since the 1983 discovery of a large radar under

---

*Another gray area of the treaty, and one of greater practical significance in the near term, concerns the upgrading of antiaircraft defenses to enable them to intercept tactical or intermediate-range ballistic missiles. Both the Soviet SA-12 and the U.S. Patriot air defense systems are expected to have the ATBM (anti-tactical ballistic missile) capability, and the SA-12 has reportedly been tested in such a role. ATBMs are implicitly permitted under the treaty, which defines an ABM as a system "to counter strategic ballistic missiles or their elements in flight trajectory." But while an ATBM would not pose a threat to intercontinental-range missiles, it would have some inherent capability to intercept submarine-launched ballistic missiles. For this reason, and because they promise to aggravate existing ambiguities about compliance with treaty restrictions on the upgrading of air defenses and their testing in an "ABM mode," ATBMs are a serious threat to the treaty's future effectiveness.[15]

construction near Abalakova in Siberia, in the vicinity of Soviet ICBM fields. In a January 1984 report alleging Soviet violations of a number of arms control agreements, the Reagan administration cited this radar as "almost certainly" a violation of the ABM Treaty.

The purpose of the Abalakova radar is not clear. The Soviets have declared that it is a space tracking facility, which would be consistent with the treaty. While this claim is difficult to disprove, many observers have concluded that the radar is more likely meant to fill a gap in the Soviet early warning radar network. If this is the case, the radar's location some 500 miles inside the Soviet border would violate the treaty. Because early warning radars are assumed to have some BMD battle-management potential, the treaty requires that they be located on the periphery of the national territory (where they are highly vulnerable), and be oriented outward.

In response to the American allegations, the Soviet Union has charged that a U.S. early warning radar network, called PAVE PAWS, is being upgraded to a BMD capability. Two new PAVE PAWS installations to be constructed in Texas and Georgia are reported to have 240-degree coverage, enabling them to cover significant portions of the continental United States. These radar are in keeping with the treaty's requirements as to location, however, and do not appear to raise as serious a compliance question as the Abalakova installation.

A number of other past and present Soviet BMD activities, including an alleged rapid-reload test of a new Soviet interceptor missile, have reportedly been questioned by the United States. As far as can be judged from the public record, however, no violations have been charged. Most questions of this nature are inherently difficult to resolve, due to technical complexities and ambiguities in treaty language. In several past instances, Soviet activities were either discontinued or explained to the satisfaction of U.S. officials after being raised before the United States-Soviet Standing Consultative Commission. The Abalakova radar is the only alleged ABM Treaty violation mentioned in the January 1984 administration report.[16]

The possibility of Soviet violations is of serious concern and should be pursued diligently by the United States. It is important to bear in mind, however, that none of the activities in question poses a militarily significant threat. Given the technical difficulties facing BMD, available evidence does not suggest that the Soviets are preparing a "breakout" from the treaty. There is reason to believe the Soviets value the treaty as a way of containing superior American technology. From this standpoint, the Soviets are probably anxious to forestall the kind of BMD competition that a breakdown of the treaty would stimulate. Soviet advocacy of a moratorium on ASAT testing tends to support this interpretation.*

---

*Although Reagan administration officials sometimes credit the Soviet Union with a large lead over the United States in directed energy space weapons, very little specific information is available on Soviet programs in this area. The Soviets are as unlikely as the United States to achieve a breakthrough leading to an effective space-based missile defense. Additional cause for doubting the potential for Soviet breakthrough in space-based BMD is the historical record of Soviet operational difficulties with space systems. The Soviets have generally proven unable to attain high standards of reliability and longevity with their space platforms, particularly those involving extensive automation. In light of this experience, it is questionable whether the Soviets could develop an effective space laser even for ASAT missions, much less for the enormously more demanding BMD role.

One thing seems certain, however: there can be little hope of resolving questions about Soviet compliance with the ABM Treaty so long as the United States maintains a presidential-level commitment to a major BMD effort. America cannot have it both ways—pursuing a goal that is clearly in conflict with the treaty while invoking the treaty against Soviet BMD activities.

The administration has attempted to reconcile this contradiction by asserting its BMD program "can be fully pursued for the next several years within existing treaty constraints."[17] This claim is disingenuous in two ways. First, it is not clear that even the near-term activities planned by the United States can be reconciled with the ABM Treaty. At the very least, planned demonstrations of technologies such as a space-based pointing and tracking system and an airborne sensor will move the United States deep into gray areas of the treaty.[18] Second, a political commitment to the pursuit of a BMD breakthrough could make the technical issue of near-term compliance irrelevant by signaling to the Soviet Union that abrogation of the treaty in the future is likely. In these circumstances, the treaty could be dead well before the United States crosses the line of clearly proscribed activities.

EFFECTS ON THE ATLANTIC ALLIANCE

An American commitment to ballistic defense would cause major political and strategic strains within the

Judging from previous Soviet experience, repair and maintenance demands would probably necessitate that any such Soviet weapon be deployed on a staffed platform. See Steven Meyer, "Soviet Military Programs and the 'New High Ground,' " *Survival,* September–October, 1983.

Atlantic Alliance. European apprehensions about the Strategic Defense Initiative have already been expressed in NATO meetings during 1984, and would certainly grow if the United States moved toward actual deployment of missile defenses and abandonment of the ABM Treaty. This unease has several sources.

First, Great Britain and France have a direct self-interest in the ABM Treaty. Their own relatively small nuclear forces could be threatened with obsolescence by an expanded Soviet BMD. If the superpowers begin to deploy substantial missile defenses, Britain and France (as well as China) will feel compelled to expand and modernize their nuclear forces to assure their continued ability to retaliate in response to a Soviet attack. In these circumstances, the prospects for an arms control agreement covering theater nuclear forces in Europe would become even bleaker than they are now. The Soviet Union, which walked out of the "Euromissile" talks in late 1983 following the first deployments of U.S. cruise and Pershing II missiles, insists that French and British forces be taken into account in such an agreement. The willingness of France and Britain to participate in an agreement limiting their nuclear forces, however, would be very doubtful in the context of new Soviet BMD deployments. France has stated explicitly that among its conditions for participation in future Euromissile talks is that "defensive systems . . . must remain limited."[19]

Beyond the specific interests of France and Britain in the BMD issue, there is a widespread concern in Europe generally about the effect of a U.S. missile defense program on East-West relations and the arms control process. In Germany, the country most sensitive to the state of East-West relations, American talk of ballistic missile defense has produced a rare consensus among political leaders. West German Defense Minister Manfred Woerner has declared that American efforts to develop BMD could "destabilize the East-West balance" and dramatically increase tensions with Moscow. Karsten Voigt, foreign policy spokesman for the Social Democrat opposition, predicted the U.S. space weapons program could set off a storm of public protests and trigger a serious confrontation between West Germany and the United States. At the other end of the political spectrum, Franz Josef Strauss, head of the conservative Christian Socialist Union, denounced the Reagan administration's Star Wars program as a unilateral rejection of the United States-European partnership and a threat the survival of the Alliance.[20]

Europeans also fear that BMD signifies a retreat into a "Fortress America" mentality, which could sacrifice important European interests for the sake of greater American security. In the opinion of Dutch Defense Minister Jacob de Ruiter, it makes Europeans uneasy that a missile defense system protecting the United States would leave Europe vulnerable.[21] Other Europeans have taken this argument a step further, worrying aloud that a partially protected United States might be more willing to risk war with the Soviet Union, a war that would almost surely result in Europe's destruction.

U.S. officials have attempted to respond to these fears by assuring NATO leaders that an American missile defense program would include protection of Europe against tactical and intermediate-range Soviet missiles.[22] The technical obstacles to defending Europe, however, are even more formidable than those confronting a defense of U.S. territory. Thousands of "battlefield" nuclear weapons are deployed on European soil, and NATO policy calls for the West to resort to the first use of nuclear weapons if confronted by a Soviet offensive that cannot be halted with conventional forces. In a Soviet nuclear attack on Western Europe, moreover, many if not most of the weapons would be delivered by aircraft. For these reasons, Europe could not hope to escape nuclear devastation in the event of war, even with highly effective missile defenses in place.

SUMMARY

The superficial attractions of a strategy of nuclear defense disappear when the overall consequences of BMD deployments are considered. More than any foreseeable offensive arms breakthrough, defenses would radically transform the context of U.S.-Soviet nuclear relations, setting in motion a chain of events and reactions that would leave both superpowers much less secure and could even lead to nuclear war. Deterrence would be weakened and crisis instability increased. Damage limitation would be undermined by a greater emphasis on the targeting of cities and the increased vulnerability of command and control systems. And virtually the entire arms control process would be swept away by the abrogation of the ABM Treaty, the launching of a new offensive round of the arms race, and the extension of the arms race into space. Finally, a commitment to BMD would provoke a serious crisis in the Atlantic Alliance.

The late Republican Senator Arthur Vandenberg

was fond of attacking schemes he opposed by declaring "the end unattainable, the means harebrained, and the cost staggering." For Vandenberg, this was a politically useful form of exaggeration. For total ballistic missile defense, it is an entirely fitting description.

PART III
Anti-Satellite Weapons

9:
OVERVIEW OF
ANTI-SATELLITE WEAPONS

Satellites give the United States prompt, precise, and irreplaceable intelligence about Soviet strategic forces. They provide an invaluable view of many other aspects of Soviet military capabilities and activities. In a crisis they would allow each side to watch the movements of the other, and thereby to gauge its objectives and apprehensions. If hostilities were ever to break out between the superpowers, whatever hope there would be for controlling the conflict and bringing it to an early end would rest largely on satellite surveillance, on the command of strategic forces via satellites, and on satellite communication between the adversaries.

But satellites are two-edged swords. They have a beneficial role in arms control, confidence building, and conflict resolution, but their unique ability to see, to hear, and to communicate greatly amplifies the effectiveness of the military forces that they serve. As a result, they become exceptionally tempting targets as soon as hostilities are about to begin.

In the 1960s both the United States and the Soviet

Union fielded systems having anti-satellite (ASAT) capabilities. The United States eventually dismantled its ASAT systems, and adopted the position that its national security would be best served by abstaining from competition in ASAT weaponry. The Soviet Union, on the other hand, continued sporadic testing of a rather primitive device that can attack objects in low earth orbits.

By the latter part of the 1970s the United States altered its approach, though a weapon-free space environment continued to be its goal.[1] The new tactics had both a military and a diplomatic component: a program to develop a satellite interceptor and simultaneous negotiations toward a treaty that would ban the testing and deployment of ASAT weapons. These negotiations did not reach fruition in the last administration,[2] and have not been pursued since then.[3] In the interim, both superpowers' ASAT programs have continued apace.[4]

In August 1981 the Soviet Union submitted to the United Nations a draft treaty calling for a "prohibition on the stationing of weapons of any kind in outer space." The United States did not respond to this initiative, despite prodding from a number of senators. On May 18, 1983, a draft ASAT test ban treaty was presented by this panel at a hearing before the Senate Armed Services Committee. Three months later the Soviet Union submitted "A Treaty on the Prohibition of the Use of Force in Outer Space or from Space Against the Earth" to the United Nations. The newer Soviet treaty has considerable overlap with the UCS draft, a fact that has been acknowledged by influential Soviet spokesmen.

Congressional concern about ASAT negotiations

mounted in the following months and culminated in a provision in the Defense Appropriations Act for Fiscal Year 1984 that restricted ASAT funding unless the president provided a report to Congress specifying the steps that he contemplated undertaking toward ASAT arms control. In compliance with this provision, the administration issued a report on March 31, 1984, stating that "no arrangements or agreements beyond those already governing military activities in outer space have been found to date that are judged to be in the overall interest of the United States and its allies," and that it would not "be productive to engage in formal international negotiations."

The United States has therefore adopted a new strategy of ongoing confrontation for protecting its space assets. An era of strenuous competition in space weaponry will begin, and even if one competitor does on occasion enjoy a fleeting advantage, the national security of both rivals will inexorably erode. Any threat to satellites, whether real or potential, will undermine confidence in the ability to deter attack. By the same token, an awareness that satellites are at risk will tend to destabilize a crisis. Even in times of peace, a keen rivalry in the development and testing of ASAT weapons is certain to cause friction, increase suspicions, undermine confidence in the ability to deter attack, and perhaps inadvertently spark a conflict.

The absence of any limitations on ASATs will also allow an anti-ballistic missile development program to masquerade as an ASAT program, in order to evade the ban on space-based ABMs of Article V of the ABM Treaty. As stated in that treaty, ballistic missile defense (BMD) undermines the deterrent value of an opponent's ICBM force. Therefore even a minimal and ineffective BMD capability or an ASAT system that was not intended to have a BMD role could be misperceived as a serious threat and trigger buildups of offensive missiles. Furthermore, if space-based BMD is pursued, the high-altitude satellites that provide early warning of missile attack and command the strategic nuclear forces will be threatened with prompt destruction. This could occur even if the space-based BMD system does not provide a viable defense against large-scale strategic attacks.

It does not take great powers of prophecy to predict this erosion of security, for the analogy with the history of MIRV technology is both instructive and disturbing. In that case, the Soviet Union failed to foresee that the United States would develop MIRVs as a sophisticated response to a primitive ballistic-missile defense of Moscow. Neither did the United States anticipate that the strategic benefit that it achieved with MIRVs would eventually boomerang by putting at risk U.S. silo-based missiles. Today, finally, there is a broad consensus that strategic stability and alliance cohesion would have fared better had the United States abstained from introducing MIRVs. Nevertheless, there is a strange reluctance to recognize that this painful lesson applies directly to current trends in the arms competition in space.

It is in the long-term interest of both superpowers to minimize the likelihood of conflict in space. This is especially true for the United States. Some Soviet satellites do pose a direct threat to certain U.S. military forces, but these threats can be countered without ASATs. Because the United States is more dependent on space-based systems than the Soviet Union, it is on balance better for the United States to constrain the potential threat from Soviet ASATs than to prepare to attack Soviet satellites. Such constraints can be achieved only by negotiations that build on the established body of international law represented by the Test Ban Treaty, which forbids nuclear explosions in outer space; the Outer Space Treaty, which bans space-based weapons of mass destruction; and the ABM Treaty, which bans space-based ABM systems and protects satellites serving as "national means of verification."

It is the purpose of this report to examine the feasibility of negotiated limits on anti-satellite weapons. To this end, we compare the current status and potential capabilities of the U.S. and Soviet ASAT systems, and assess the military significance of the threat posed by these weapons. We find that:

1. The tested Soviet ground-based ASAT presents a rather unreliable, inflexible and ponderous threat to a small number of U.S. satellites in low orbits but does not threaten high-orbit early-warning navigation and communication satellites essential to the strategic forces.

2. The U.S. ASAT, which is launched by an F-15 aircraft, if it performs according to specifications in impending flight tests, will present a prompt and flexible threat to the majority of Soviet satellites, which are in low orbits, and a limited threat to Soviet early-warning and communication satellites in highly elliptical orbits.

3. The U.S. ASAT technology demonstrated in June 1984 when a dummy ICBM warhead was successfully intercepted in space is more than a match for the capability shown by the Soviet ASAT. It can no

longer be claimed that the Soviets have a tested nonnuclear ASAT while the United States does not.

We therefore conclude that the existing ASAT capabilities do not yet present a serious threat to either superpower; that it is essential for the security of the United States to restrict the further growth of those capabilities; that negotiations toward that objective are feasible; and that it is urgent to begin such negotiations promptly.

To focus attention on issues that are likely to arise in such negotiations, we have put forward an explicit treaty text. In view of our assessment of the current situation and its implications for the future, our draft treaty is first and foremost a ban on the testing of ASAT weapons. In essence, *the draft treaty requires that no weapon that can destroy, damage, or change the flight trajectory of space objects can be tested in space or against space objects.* Furthermore, the treaty obligates the parties to begin negotiations toward a prohibition on possession of ASATs as soon as the test ban is in place. The proposed text is for a bilateral treaty, because the accession of the Soviet Union and the United States is a prerequisite to a multilateral accord and because U.S. security depends primarily on constraining Soviet capabilities.

We examine the problem of verifying compliance with such an ASAT test ban and conclude that the hazards of a totally uninhibited competition in space weaponry are far greater than the potential threat posed by the tightly constrained evolution of ASAT capability that may be possible because of ambiguities in verification. Furthermore, we show that these residual risks can be reduced to an acceptable level by satellite defense measures (such as decoy satellites, maneuverability, etc.) that would cost much less than the program necessary if there were no negotiated constraints. These conclusions show that it is on the whole easier to detect violations of the treaty than to determine, in the absence of a treaty, which of an enormous array of permitted space activities pose a security threat.

Finally, on the basis of our findings, we argue that it would be advantageous for the United States to agree to an immediate moratorium on further ASAT space tests and that the security of the United States would not be in jeopardy should such negotiations fail or should a treaty be abrogated or circumvented by the Soviet Union.

10:

CURRENT U.S. AND SOVIET SPACE ASSETS AND ASAT SYSTEMS

Negotiations toward restraints on further ASAT development must take into account the existing balance in U.S. and Soviet space assets and military capabilities.

SATELLITES

Military satellites have a large variety of missions. The nature of the mission is a major factor in determining the type of orbit that is used, which in turn determines the vulnerability of the satellite to ASAT attack. The orbital characteristics, endurance, and missions of the major U.S. and Soviet military satellite networks will be found in Tables 3 and 4 and Figure 19.

Satellites in low orbits, whose altitudes range up to roughly 1,600 km, are most suitable for the detection of visual and infrared radiation from the earth and provide the most detailed images of the earth's surface. Photoreconnaissance, ocean surveillance, and most electronics intelligence (ELINT) satellites are in low orbits. For communication between widely separated points and for surveillance of broad areas, a geosynchronous orbit is preferable, for such a satellite hovers above a fixed point on the equator at an altitude of about 35,000 km. U.S. satellites that provide early warning of missile firings by detecting the heat radiation from the booster's flame are in geosynchronous orbits, as are most U.S. communications satellites.

Satellites can also be in highly elliptical orbits that dip as low as several hundred kilometers in the Southern Hemisphere, and rise in the Northern Hemisphere as high as geosynchronous satellites. Because the Soviets have important facilities in the Arctic, they exploit such "Molniya" orbits for their early warning and many of their communications satellites. The U.S. SDS satellites, which handle communications with forces in the Arctic, are also in Molniya orbits. Both nations are deploying constellations of navigation satellites in semi-synchronous orbits at altitudes of about 19,000 km. The U.S. global positioning system (GPS) may be used in conjunction with a suitable receiver carried in an infantryman's pack, a helicopter, a ship, or a missile. The satellites in this system will provide a highly accurate determination of position and velocity under all weather conditions, which all U.S. military forces will be able to exploit. GPS will also carry IONDS, the integrated operational nuclear detection system, which will be able to measure the yield and location of nuclear explosions with much greater precision than is currently possible.

There are significant differences between the military satellite fleets of the two superpowers. Satellites essential to U.S. strategic forces in wartime—early-warning, nuclear attack assessment, communications, and navigation—are almost all in high orbits where they are not vulnerable to the current generation of Soviet ASATs.

Figure 19. *Typical Distribution of U.S. and Soviet Satellites by Altitude and Mission.*

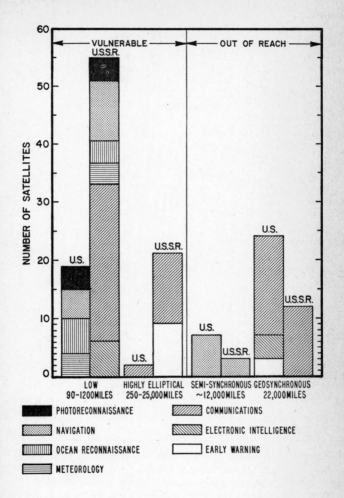

Table 3. United States Military Satellite Systems

Mission	Class	Initiated	'82 Launches
Communication	DSCS II	1971	1
	DSCS III	1982	1
	SDS	1971	0
	FLTSATCOM	1978	0
	NATO	1970	0
	MARISAT	1976	0
	LES	1965	0
	AFSATCOM***		
Navigation	Transit	1964	0
	NOVA	1981	0
	NTS	1974	0
	NAVSTAR	1978	0
Meteorology	NOAA	1970	0
	DMSP	1971	1
Early warning	DSP	1970	1
Nuclear explosion detection°	Vela Hotel	1963	0
Electronics intelligence	Rhyolite	1973	0
Ocean reconnaissance	NOSS	1976	0
Photographic intelligence	Key-Hole (KH-9)	##	0
	Big Bird	1971	1
	KH-11	1976	2
Geodesy	GEOS-3	1975	0
	LAGEOS	1976	0

G = Geosynchronous orbit: Satellite moves with same period as the Earth
    at an altitude of approximately 35,600 km.
= Statistic uncertain or unavailable using unclassified literature.
* = DSCS III is follow-on to DSCS II; same complement is planned.
** = NOVA satellites are being incorporated into the Transit network.
*** = AFSATCOM equipment is housed on "host" SDS, FLTSATCOM,
    LES, and DSCS III satellites.
@ = NAVSTAR plans call for a network of 18 operational satellites and
    three spares by 1988.
Apogee = Highest known point of orbit above the earth, given in km.

Complement	Inclination	Period	Perigee	Apogee	Lifespan
4 + 2	2.0	G	G	G	5 years
*	2.5	G	G	G	10 years
2	63.5	700	250	39,300	2 years
4 + 1	2.0	G	G	G	5 years
3	2.8	G	G	G	7 years
3	2.5	G	G	G	10 years
##	25.0	G	G	G	#
5	90.0	105	1,075	1,100	#
**	90.0	110	1,170	1,190	6 years
(1)	125.1	468	13,440	13,770	#
6 @	63.0	720	20,200	20,300	5–7 years
2	99.0	102	810	860	18 months
2	99.0	102	810	870	3 years
3	2.0	G	G	G	2–5 years
2	32.5	6730	110,900	112,200	10+ years
4	0.2	G	G	G	3–6 years
6	63.4	107	1040	1170	##
(1)	96.5	##	52	119	6 weeks
(1)	96.0	89	150	330	3–5 months
2	97.0	93	220	550	2+ years
##	115.0	102	840	855	##
##	110.0	225	5840	5950	##

° = Other nuclear explosion detection sensors are aboard DSP and SDS satellites. The NAVSTAR system will house an advanced nuclear explosion detection system called IONDS beginning with NAVSTAR-8. Soviet nuclear detection sensors are most likely on their early warning and/or Molniya communication satellites.

Complement = Indicates the nominal number of satellites in a given network; + designates spares in orbit; ( ) = uncertain complement.

Inclination = Highest latitude reached N and S, given in degrees.

Period = Time it takes to complete one orbit, given in minutes.

Perigee = Lowest altitude of same orbit as apogee, also given in km.

Table 4. Soviet Military Satellite Systems

Mission	Class	Initiated	'82 Launches
Communication	Com 1	1970	4
	Com 2	1970	2 @
	Molniya 1	1965	4
	Molniya 3	1974	2
	Raduga	1975	1
	Gorizont	1978	2
Navigation	Nav 2	1974	6
	Nav 3	1976	2
	GLONASS*	1982	3
Meteorology	METEOR 1	1969	0
	METEOR 2	1975	2
Early warning	EW-1	1972	5
Electronics intelligence	ELINT 2	1970	4
Ocean reconnaissance	EORSAT	1979	5
	RORSAT	1967	4
Photographic intelligence	Low Resolution	1962	3
	Med Resolution	1968	8
	HI Resolution-1	1963	23
	HI Resolution-2	1975	1
Geodesy	Geod-1	1968	0

G, ## = See footnotes beneath Table 3.

* = GLONASS will be a navigation network similar to the U.S. NAVSTAR system; 9–12 operational satellites are expected.

@ = Com 2 satellites are launched in octets by a single carrier rocket.

Complement	Inclination	Period	Perigee	Apogee	Lifespan
3	74.1	101	790	810	17 month
24	74.0	115	1385	1565	5 month
8	62.9	718	400	39,900	2 year
4	62.9	718	400	39,900	2 year
2 + 2	0.3	G	G	G	##
##	0.8	G	G	G	##
6	82.9	105	965	1020	16 month
4	82.9	105	965	1020	3 year
3	64.8	673	19,075	19,075	##
(1)	98.0	98	630	680	##
(3)	82.5	104	870	940	##
9	62.8	718	400	40,000	20 month
6	81.2	97	620	640	20 month
(2)	65.0	93	425	445	6 month
(2)	65.0	90	250	265	3–4 month
(1)	82.3	89	210	250	2 week
(1)	70.3	92	350	450	2 week
(1)	65–80	89	170	360	2 week
(1)	65–70	89	170	370	6 week
##	3.0	109	1140	1430	##

Electronics intelligence (ELINT) satellites detect and intercept foreign communications and radar signals.

Geodetic satellites gather precise information about the earth's gravitational and magnetic fields; this information is used to improve missile guidance.

When the GPS satellite constellation is completed in several years, all these U.S. satellites will be in safe orbits. The U.S. imaging and ELINT satellites in low and vulnerable orbits are essential to monitoring of treaty compliance and to surveillance of all sorts of Soviet military activities. As a result, these more vulnerable satellites are of primary importance in peacetime, for crisis management, and in conventional (non-nuclear) military operations, which are becoming increasingly dependent on the intelligence data provided by such satellites. In contrast to the United States, the Soviet Union's satellites are predominantly in low or highly elliptical orbits, spending all or part of their time within range of low-altitude interceptors.

U.S. satellites are considerably more sophisticated, more reliable, and far more long-lived than Soviet satellites. For example, the Soviet Union has only recently begun to retrieve high-resolution film capsules without returning the satellite to the ground, a technique that the United States has been using since the early 1960s.[5] It is only within the last few years that the Soviets have been able to bring their early-warning satellites to operational status.[6] Despite a large commitment to ocean surveillance from space, for example, malfunctions reportedly prevented Soviet satellites from monitoring the Falkland war.[7]

These differences between the two satellite fleets are not just a reflection of superior U.S. technology. They also reflect the quite different geopolitical environment faced by each nation. The closed nature of Soviet society has led the United States to invest heavily in satellites that can provide prompt and comprehensive data about as wide a variety of Soviet activities as possible. Since U.S. forces are spread across the globe, secure long-range communications are also essential to U.S. security. For that reason, more than 60 percent of long-haul military communications are now transmitted via satellites, and the percentage is growing. There is no possibility of developing facilities on the earth's surface that could provide a satisfactory replacement for this satellite system.

The Soviet Union's military forces are mainly on or near to the Eurasian land mass and can readily communicate by using a large variety of ground-based and airborne facilities in addition to satellites. Indeed, the Soviet Union evidently uses its satellites as a backup for its communications and intelligence-gathering systems that are ground-based and airborne, while the converse is true of the United States.[8]

U.S. Defense Department publications claim that the Soviets have a much larger space program than the United States and cite the far larger number of Soviet launches and the payload placed into orbit as evidence for this claim.[9] But the disparity in launch frequency is entirely accounted for by the much shorter life span of Soviet satellites or by the need to retrieve satellites.[10] Of the 101 Soviet satellites launched during 1982, more than 50 percent were no longer in orbit or were out of operation by year's end.[11] Figure 20 documents this assertion in detail for the case of photoreconnaissance, where Soviet satellites typically stay aloft for two weeks, while U.S. KH-11 satellites stay up for more than two years.[12] Furthermore, a comparison of gross weight placed into orbit should include the weight of the Shuttle orbiter; three Shuttle flights exceed the 300,000 kg annually put into orbit by the Soviet Union.

The notion that the scope of the Soviet space program can be gauged by estimates of the Soviet space

Figure 20. *Coverage by U.S. and Soviet Long-Lived Photographic Reconnaissance Satellites during 1977–83.* Each block represents one satellite. The beginning of each block corresponds to the date the satellite was launched, and the length of the block corresponds to the lifetime of the satellite in days.
SOURCE: Stockholm International Peace Research Institute

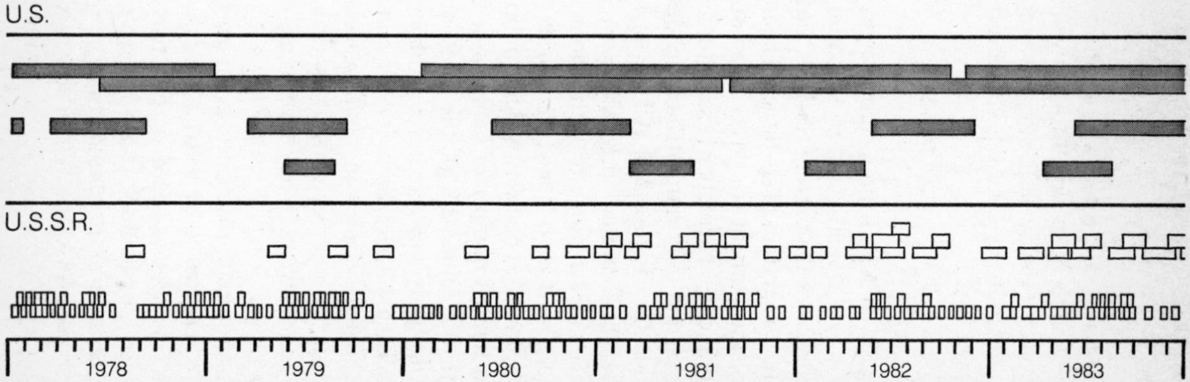

U.S.
U.S.S.R.
1978
1979
1980
1981
1982
1983

budget should also be treated with caution. If such a comparison were made in agriculture, it would lead to the conclusion that the Soviet Union has a more potent food-producing industry than the United States, quite contrary to reality.

ASATS

The existing Soviet ASAT interceptor weighs 2,800 kg. It is launched by a ground-based SS-9 booster (the very large predecessor of the current SS-18 ICBM booster) into an orbit close to that of its target. The interceptor then crosses the path of its target after one or two orbital revolutions, whereupon its non-nuclear warhead explodes, and the resultant shrapnel destroys the target satellite (see Figure 21). All Soviet tests have used launchers at Tyuratam in Kazakhstan, and orbits within a very narrow range of inclinations (62 to 65 degrees). Because it is so heavy, the Soviet ASAT requires a very powerful booster, which can be launched from only a limited number of facilities in the Soviet Union. With the retirement of the SS-9, operational Soviet silos probably would require modifications to be used as ASAT launch sites. Since it is difficult to launch large liquid-fueled boosters in rapid succession from the same pad, the number of ASATs that could be launched by the Soviets in any given time interval is highly constrained.

The highest altitude reached thus far by the Soviet interceptor is reported to be about 2,300 km. Since the Soviet ASAT is ground-based, it can only attack a satellite whose ground track runs close to the ASAT launch site. Because of the earth's rotation, this occurs twice a day, so the ASAT must wait some six hours on average to attack a particular target satellite.

Knowledgeable observers estimate that the Soviet Union would require well in excess of a week to destroy all the low-orbit U.S. satellites that are within its ASAT's range. Many factors enter into this estimate: the fact that the ASAT is launched from the ground, the paucity of suitable launch sites, the liquid-fueled booster, and the poor performance of the Soviet ASAT in tests.

The only U.S. satellites that have inclinations similar to those used in the Soviet ASAT tests are ocean-reconnaissance satellites (NOSS) and the SDS communication satellites. The latter are in highly elliptical orbits, move more rapidly at low altitudes than the Soviet orbital ASAT, and are therefore difficult to intercept. All other U.S. communications satellites are in geosynchronous orbits and provide ample facilities for communication by themselves. These facts have led many observers to wonder whether the Soviet ASAT may be primarily intended for attacking Chinese, rather than American, satellites. This speculation is supported by notable similarities between the orbits used by Chinese satellites and the Soviet ASAT, and by correlations in timing between Chinese satellite launches and Soviet ASAT tests. Nevertheless, the Soviet ASAT could threaten U.S. photoreconnaissance satellites in low-altitude polar orbits.

It appears difficult for the Soviets to modify their ASAT system enough to threaten targets in high orbits. If the Soviet ASAT were to reach a satellite in geosynchronous orbit, it would have to be given an additional velocity of 4 kilometers per second, which would require an additional stage of propulsion about four times larger than the enormous booster that it already uses to reach low orbits. That is why the current Soviet system

Figure 21. *Soviet ASAT Approaching and Destroying Its Target.* The Soviet ASAT goes into orbit, homes on its target satellite by radar, and its warhead then explodes, destroying the target with pellets.

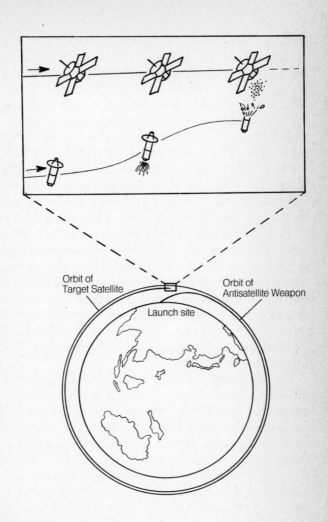

Orbit of
Target Satellite

Orbit of
Antisatellite Weapon

Launch site

threatens only low-orbit space objects. About a third of all U.S. satellites fall into this category, and their most important national security functions are photographic and electronic surveillance of the earth's surface. Those critical U.S. satellites responsible for early warning, nuclear attack assessment, additional electronic intelligence, and military communications are in very high orbits and not vulnerable to the current Soviet ASAT.

The American anti-satellite system is based on quite different principles: it is not designed to go into orbit but to intercept its quarry by "direct ascent," a far more challenging approach requiring extreme accuracy in position and time. The interceptor is the so-called miniature homing vehicle (MHV), which is carried into space on a two-stage rocket that in turn is launched from a high-altitude F-15 fighter plane (Figure 24). The MHV is a small cylinder with a diameter of about 30 centimeters that seeks its target by a combination of infrared telescopes, a laser gyroscope, and a set of small jets that can alter its trajectory. It destroys by direct impact at very high velocity.

Because it is plane-borne, the U.S. ASAT is in principle able to operate from any airbase that has adequate communication facilities. Midair refueling and carrier-based planes could provide the United States with global ASAT coverage. Interception of all Soviet satellites in low orbits could take place within a matter of hours if enough ASAT-bearing planes were suitably dispersed, and if extensive ground or satellite facilities for command and control were installed. Soviet satellites in highly elliptical orbits are also vulnerable to the U.S. ASAT if the weapon is based in the Southern Hemisphere. Present procurement plans call for only two squadrons of ASAT-equipped F-15s at Langley Air

Force Base in Virginia and McChord Air Force Base in the state of Washington, but the ultimate capabilities of the system are a matter of operational choice.

The U.S. ASAT could not be used to destroy the Soviet ASAT itself. Tethered decoys could readily be attached to the Soviet ASAT for the duration of its flight, which could misdirect the MHV. In its present form, the MHV cannot reach geosynchronous satellites, but this is not of great consequence at this time, because almost all Soviet satellites are in low or highly elliptical orbits.

By using a three-stage booster the U.S. ASAT should be able to attack geosynchronous targets. The whole system would weigh some 7,300 kg and could still be carried on an F-15. On the other hand, it is not clear whether the MHV would have the ability to home on such a remote target. Furthermore, the military value of such a system is questionable, since it would take many hours for the interceptor to reach a geosynchronous satellite. There would be ample warning for bringing backup facilities into operation, and for evasive action by the target satellite if it had been equipped for that purpose.

The first flight test of the U.S. ASAT took place on January 21, 1984. An F-15 launched the ASAT booster rocket against a point in space, but without a homing vehicle aboard. The Defense Department has not revealed whether this test was successful. Further tests will involve the MHV, and will eventually include orbiting targets. The system is scheduled to reach operational status in 1987.

The Soviet ASAT has been tested some twenty times since 1968. In the first test series (1968–71), radar hom-

Figure 22. *American ASAT Approaching and Destroying Its Target.* The miniature homing vehicle is launched from the F-15 fighter and is boosted directly toward its target by a two-stage rocket. The target satellite is destroyed by direct impact. For the uppermost sketch, the size of the homing vehicle is exaggerated for the sake of clarity.

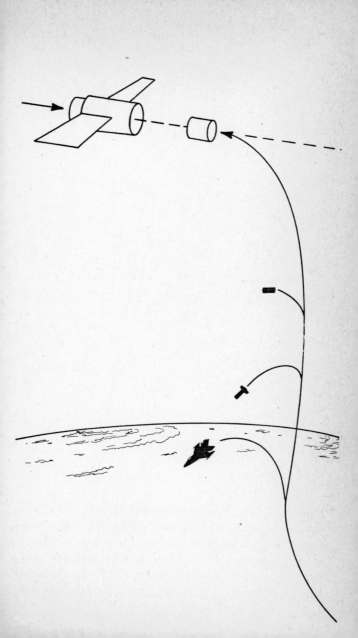

Figure 23. *U.S. Miniature Homing Vehicle.* This "kill vehicle" is launched from an F-15 fighter atop a two-stage rocket toward its target. The homing vehicle seeks the warm satellite against the cold background of space by using its infrared sensors and telescopes. The device is a cylinder about 30 centimeters in diameter and 30 centimeters long.

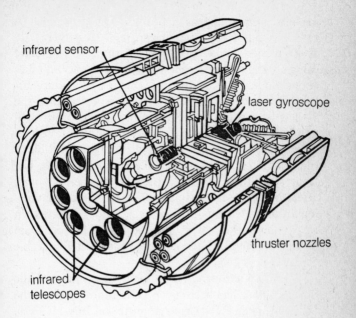

infrared sensor

laser gyroscope

thruster nozzles

infrared
telescopes

ing was used to approach the target, and the success rate was quite high (approximately 70 percent). A radar homer could be jammed if the target satellite carries a jammer; interception in the second orbit takes about three hours, providing ample opportunity for evasive maneuvering. It has been reported that the Soviets later tested interception in the first orbit, with two successes in four tries; they have also tested an optical/infrared homer that would not be susceptible to radar jamming, but this has failed in all six trials. The last test on June 18, 1982, received considerable press attention because it was part of a large exercise involving various elements of the Soviet strategic forces. In this instance, the optical/infrared homer failed.[13] Data on the Soviet ASAT test program is collected in Table 5 and Figure 24.

The most authoritative military assessment of the Soviet ASAT has been given in testimony before the Senate Foreign Relations Committee on July 11, 1979, by General Lew Allen, then Air Force chief of staff.

I think our general opinion is that we give it a very questionable operational capability for a few launches. In other words, it is a threat that we are worried about, but they have not had a test program that would cause us to believe it is a very credible threat.

Since the day that statement was made, the Soviets have held four further tests. The only success was with the old system using the radar homer to intercept in the second orbit, the technique that had performed reasonably well at the time of General Allen's testimony. The three failures employed the potentially more lethal optical/infrared homer. As a result, the 1979 assessment by the Air Force chief of staff should still be valid today.

Table 5. Soviet ASAT Tests

Test	Date	Intercept Altitude (km)	Orbits Before Intercept	Test Result
1	October 20, 1968	525	2	Failure
2	November 1, 1968	535	2	Success
3	October 23, 1970	530	2	Failure
4	October 30, 1970	535	2	Success
5	February 25, 1971	585	2	Success
6	April 4, 1971	1,005	2	Success
7	December 3, 1971	230	2	Success
8	February 16, 1976	575	1	Failure
9	April 13, 1976	590	1	Success
10	July 21, 1976	1,630	2	Failure
11	December 27, 1976	570	2	Failure
12	May 23, 1977	1,710	1	Failure
13	June 17, 1977	1,575	1	Success
14	October 26, 1977	150	2	Success
15	December 21, 1977	995	2	Failure
16	May 19, 1978	985	2	Failure
17	April 18, 1980	1,000	2	Failure
18	February 2, 1981	1,005	2	Failure
19	March 14, 1981	1,005	2	Success
20	June 18, 1982	1,005	2	Failure

Test results for the anti-satellite weapon system adopted by the USSR are summarized in this table.

Figure 24. *Soviet ASAT Tests.*
SOURCE: N. Johnson, *The Soviet Year in Space,* 1982.

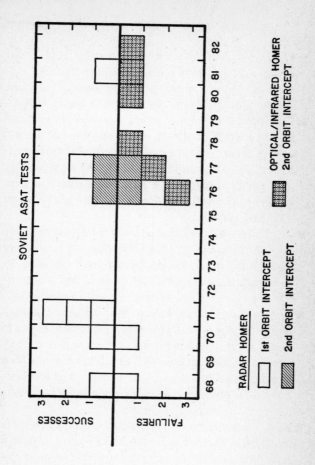

SOVIET ASAT TESTS

RADAR HOMER

1st ORBIT INTERCEPT

2nd ORBIT INTERCEPT

OPTICAL/INFRARED HOMER

2nd ORBIT INTERCEPT

These facts allow us to draw up a current balance sheet:

- *The United States is more dependent on space-based military systems than the Soviet Union. For that reason and others, it has a more sophisticated, reliable, and long-lived satellite fleet than the Soviet Union.*
- *The Soviet Union has most of its satellites in vulnerable low or elliptical orbits, while the United States has a much larger proportion of its satellites in invulnerable high (or geosynchronous) orbits. The satellites U.S. strategic forces depend on in wartime are all in geosynchronous orbits, but that is not true of the Soviet Union at this time.*
- *The Soviet ASAT, though deemed to be operational by the U.S. Department of Defense, does not pose a very credible threat. It has performed poorly in tests, its homing device could easily be jammed, and it must be lofted by a massive booster from fixed launch sites.*
- *The mobile air-based U.S. system will present a more prompt and potentially more comprehensive threat to Soviet satellites if it performs in flight tests in accordance with specifications. This capability has now been demonstrated in a ground-launched test of the homing vehicle by the successful interception of a dummy warhead in its space trajectory.*
- *Both current systems are designed to attack targets in low orbits. The heavy Soviet ASAT would require a prodigious booster to carry it to geosynchronous targets. The U.S. interceptor could, with a three-stage booster, be launched from the F-15 against geosynchronous targets. On the other hand, it is not known whether it could intercept successfully at such large range, and the time required to reach its target would provide ample warning of impending attack.*

These comparisons lie behind our contention that the United States risks little if both nations' ASAT development programs were to be suspended at this time, while negotiations take place. If for one reason or another the United States should find it necessary to resume its development program, it could begin space tests promptly to bring its ASAT system up to operation standards. The Soviet ASAT system, though it is considered to be operational, poses only a rather clumsy threat to a portion of U.S. space systems; it has, moreover, little potential for attacking the warning, communication, and navigation satellites on which U.S. strategic forces depend.

In short, if negotiations fail, or arms control in space were to break down, the United States would not find itself in a disadvantageous position.

11:

TREATIES LIMITING ASAT WEAPONS

We now examine proposed treaties that seek to restrict the further development of space weapons. As mentioned previously, on May 18, 1983, three members of a panel convened under the auspices of the Union of Concerned Scientists (UCS) presented a model treaty to the Senate Foreign Relations Committee. Two years earlier, the Soviet Union had placed a draft entitled "A Treaty on the Prohibition of the Stationing of Weapons of Any Kind in Outer Space" before the United Nations. And in August 1983 the Soviet Union presented "A Treaty on the Prohibition of the Use of Force in Outer Space or from Space Against the Earth" to the United Nations. In this chapter, the UCS treaty will be compared with both Soviet proposals. The full text of the UCS treaty can be found in Appendix B.

The UCS treaty has three essential provisions:

■ The signatories would undertake not to destroy, damage, render inoperable or change the flight trajectories of space objects, and they would undertake not to place in orbit or in outer space in any manner weapons having such capabilities *or* for damaging objects in the atmosphere or on the ground.*

■ The signatories would undertake not to test weapons in space or against space objects that are for destroying, damaging, rendering inoperable, or changing the flight trajectories of space objects. Furthermore, they undertake not to test space weapons against objects in the atmosphere or on the surface of the earth.

■ Compliance would be verified by national technical means, enhanced by cooperative measures and buttressed by collateral constraints on other space activities to prevent circumvention of the treaty's provisions.

The first provision has two components: a legal confirmation that attacks on space objects are openly hostile acts; and a significant enlargement of international law, which at this time proscribes only the stationing of weapons of mass destruction in space. This second provision—the test ban—is the heart of the treaty. The third essential provision specifies that the ban is to be monitored by "national technical means," that is, by surveillance with any instruments that a signatory may wish to deploy for that purpose—whether in space or outside the borders of the other signatory—but without on-site inspection (unless agreed to in the course of operation of the treaty).

---

*The term "space objects" would correspond to "objects launched into outer space" in the Outer Space Treaty of 1967. Such objects include not only all functioning objects commonly called "satellites" but also all objects on interplanetary flights as well as all man-made pieces of debris. The term does *not* include nuclear missile warheads on ballistic trajectories, even though these pass through space. Hence, an ASAT treaty along these lines would not alter the rights or obligations of the 1972 ABM Treaty which covers weapons used against ballistic missiles.

The scope of the test ban is set by the third provision: it rules out the testing of any and all weapons against objects in space, as well as the testing of weapons in space against objects in the atmosphere or on the earth, because it is our claim that such tests are amenable to adequate verification by "national technical means." Testing of space weapons against objects on the earth or in the atmosphere is forbidden, in order to eliminate the possibility of disguising an ASAT test as the test of an antiaircraft weapon, for example. On the other hand, the treaty does not prohibit tests of weapons on the ground or in the atmosphere against objects that are not in space, because such tests could not be observed with sufficient confidence without intrusive inspection.

The treaty proposed here formulates restrictions and prohibitions in general terms. Excessive detail in an arms control accord may inadvertently leave loopholes and convey the impression that activities and weapons not explicitly prohibited are permitted. A treaty weighted down with excessive detail may also prove inflexible in coping with new circumstances and technological developments. Our purpose in presenting general treaty provisions here is to provide a focus for discussion of feasible and desirable restrictions on ASAT weapons. In actual bilateral negotiations, the United States and the Soviet Union could incorporate more detailed language into the final treaty text that reflects the best advice and wisdom that consultations within each government would provide.

The text put forward here is for a bilateral treaty. Once agreement between the United States and the Soviet Union is reached, a multilateral accord open to all nations would be desirable.

We note that our proposal is not the most comprehensive limitation on space weapons possible, for a treaty could also forbid any possession of such weapons and require that those already constructed be dismantled or destroyed. Such a comprehensive ban is what the United States evidently sought in the negotiations of 1978–79. There is much to be said in favor of such a comprehensive ban, but it also poses formidable verification problems that could be resolved only by protracted negotiations. The major difficulty in a ban on possession would probably come from the U.S. F-15 ASAT, which is small. Intrusive on-site inspection would be required to verify that it is not deployed, unless the Soviet Union was satisfied that it could acquire this knowledge by other means. While the large size of the Soviet ASAT would make the dismantling of the launchers used in past tests readily observable, it is not clear whether other launchers used in the Soviet space program could substitute for this purpose. Without on-site inspection it also would not be possible to know whether the Soviet Union retained a supply of its current ASAT interceptors, and even such inspection could not assure that interceptors were not hidden at some remote sites.

To avert further arms competition in outer space as promptly as possible, a ban on further tests of ASAT weapons in space must take priority, and the proposed treaty addresses itself to this urgent objective. Subsequent negotiations that face the knotty problems of verifying a more comprehensive ASAT ban could then be pursued in an atmosphere free of the tensions that would be created by a simultaneous competition in space weaponry. For that reason, our draft treaty obligates the parties (Article V) to begin active negotiations toward more comprehensive restrictions

Figure 25. *Comparison of U.S. and Soviet ASATs.*

The U.S. ASAT is launched at high altitude from an F-15 jet. The interceptor, which weighs 35 lbs. and is 1 foot long (see Fig. 25) is lofted into space by an 18 foot long, 2-stage rocket. The Soviet ASAT is launched by the 3-stage liquid fueled booster shown at the right to the same scale. Its payload is an explosive interceptor which weighs about 2 tons and is some 20 feet long.

U.S.

USSR

on space weapons as soon as the test ban is in place.

A ban on the use and testing in space of ASAT weapons cannot by itself protect satellites. Nevertheless, the ban on testing would erect a severe impediment to the further development of ever more capable ASAT weapons. For the foreseeable future the military and civilian branches of the United States Government will remain as dependent on satellites as they are already. It is therefore in the long-term security interest of the United States to enhance the survival of its space assets as much as possible, and to achieve this goal with as little friction, cost, and delay as it can.

We now turn to the Soviet proposals. While the Soviet draft of 1981 signaled a real interest in negotiated controls on space weapons, it suffered from a number of serious flaws. In particular, it did not explicitly forbid tests against one's own space objects. Nor did it prohibit tests from ground-based weapons against objects in space, or from weapons in space against objects in the atmosphere or on the earth. Furthermore, the 1981 draft permitted attacks on objects that were in violation of the treaty (following due notice) in case of violation. Finally, the 1981 draft appeared to sanction attacks on space objects belonging to nations that were not party to the treaty.

The new Soviet treaty has a much wider coverage, approximating that of the treaty proposed three months earlier by UCS. Soviet spokesmen, especially Academician E. P. Velikhov, have indicated that the Soviet 1983 draft derives in considerable measure from the initiative of the UCS ASAT panel. The new Soviet draft is not limited to protecting the space objects of

"States Parties" to the treaty, but rather prohibits attacks on the space objects of *any* country. Moreover, the new treaty does not by implication permit a state to destroy its own space objects, and thereby forbids the testing of satellite weapons.

Article 2, paragraph 4, of the 1983 Soviet draft sets forth an obligation on States Parties: "Not to test or create new anti-satellite systems and to destroy any anti-satellite systems that they may already have." This is a significant addition.

The new Soviet draft omits the 1981 loophole that would have permitted attacks on space objects if they had not been placed in orbit "in strict accordance with Article 1, paragraph 1" of the 1981 version.

The 1983 revision omits the earlier Soviet draft prohibition against stationing weapons of any kind in outer space, "including on reusable manned space vehicles." This specific reference, which was apparently aimed at the U.S. Space Shuttle, has been dropped. The new Soviet draft does, however, state an obligation "not to test or use manned spacecraft for military, including anti-satellite, purposes." The ambiguity of this provision may extend it beyond the proper needs of an anti-satellite treaty. If the ban on *military* uses does more than merely extend the ASAT prohibitions of the treaty to manned spacecraft, it raises very difficult problems of verification, among other things. This clause would seem to be no more acceptable to the Soviet Union than to the United States, and one should expect it to be modified or to disappear in a negotiation.

The 1983 Soviet draft parallels the UCS draft in providing for a Consultative Committee of States Parties to deal with problems of implementation. The less detailed Soviet provisions here parallel those of the

UCS draft. However, in both Article 5, paragraph 2, and Article 8 of the 1983 Soviet draft there are references to settlement of disputes under the Charter of the United Nations. An anti-satellite treaty would not of course affect the right of States Parties to resort to the United Nations, but emphasis in this treaty on United Nations settlement of disputes could create confusion and might impair the effectiveness of the treaty's consultative machinery for dealing with specialized and technical questions.

The 1983 Soviet draft remains, like its 1981 predecessor, a multilateral treaty to be negotiated and concluded among a large number of nations. The UCS draft is for a bilateral treaty, in the thought that the most expeditious and efficient way to proceed is to negotiate with the Soviet Union first, and, after securing bilateral agreement on a treaty, to open it for general adherence.

In sum, the 1983 Soviet draft represents a substantial advance. Differences remain between its provisions and those that the United States should seek in an anti-satellite treaty. These differences should be addressed in early negotiations with the Soviet Union, which has shown by its 1983 draft a serious interest in concluding an anti-satellite treaty.

12:

THE RELATIONSHIP BETWEEN ASAT AND ABM

There are two important aspects of the relationship between anti-satellite weapons and ballistic missile defense. First, what restrictions does the ABM Treaty of 1972 impose on the evolution of technologies that have an ASAT or ABM potential? Second, what is the relationship between the technologies themselves?

It has always been the position of the United States that the ABM Treaty forbids the development, testing, and deployment of ABM systems or their components, except for one system with specified equipment deployed at each nation's capital, and one system deployed in the vicinity of one ICBM field in each country. (The 1974 Protocol reduced this to one system for each side.) A recent enunciation of this position is to be found in the President's 1984 Fiscal Year Arms Control Impact Statement,[14] which appeared in April 1983, and contains the following statements:

■ The ABM Treaty bans the development, testing and deployment of all ABM systems and components that are sea-based, air-based, space-based, or mobile land-based.

■ The ABM Treaty prohibition on development, testing, and deployment of space-based ABM systems, or components for such systems, applies to directed energy [lasers and particle beams] technology (or any technology) used for this purpose. Thus, when such directed energy programs enter the field testing phase they become constrained by these ABM Treaty obligations.

■ The ballistic missile defense potential of future directed energy weapons could eventually create a conflict with the obligations assumed by the United States under the provisions of the ABM Treaty.

■ With regard to directed energy systems in an ASAT role, only the actual use of systems to interfere with national technical means used to verify compliance with strategic arms control agreements—as opposed to development, testing, or deployment of systems that could be used in such roles—is prohibited under the provisions of the ABM Treaty and the SALT I Interim Agreement and Article XV of the unratified SALT II Agreement.

In short, the ABM Treaty places severe restrictions on any weapons program that is considered to have an ABM role, whatever its physical principles or technology. On the other hand, the treaty has only a minimal impact on ASAT programs, because it only forbids interference with satellites that are used to verify strategic arms control accords.

The lack of restrictions on ASATs is the most important loophole in the ABM Treaty, since it allows claims that a weapons system under development is intended to be an ASAT when the real or potential objective is missile defense. Satellites are much more fragile than missiles, and since their time in space is measured in months or years instead of minutes, they are also far easier to target. As a result, virtually any putative BMD system will be an effective ASAT long before it achieves any significant ABM capability, and the claim that it is really only an ASAT may be difficult to refute for many years. By the same token, a program that really is intended to achieve only an ASAT capability may be perceived as an nascent BMD by the other side.

Before the president's Star Wars speech, the concerns expressed in the preceding paragraph were often viewed as far-fetched and academic. Everyone should now recognize that they are very real. Indeed, George Keyworth, the president's science advisor, while speaking of the excimer laser concept, has said that it could provide "a geosynchronous ASAT capability. It may not necessarily be the best way for the ASAT mission, but a geosynchronous ASAT capability is important to test the technology to destroy missiles." For that matter, all the space-based BMD systems discussed in this book could in all likelihood be developed into very potent ASAT systems, even though they are unlikely ever to reach the point where they would provide an effective missile defense. A directed energy weapon that is too feeble to harm a booster in the handful of minutes available for boost-phase interception could, if in the appropriate orbit, irradiate a satellite for hours on end until it achieved the intended damage. At a more mundane level, the MHV, which is the heart of the U.S. ASAT system, already displays the symbiotic relationship between ASAT and BMD: the MHV exploits technologies originally developed by the Army for its Homing Overlay project, which explored the feasibility of intercepting ICBMs in midcourse as the second tier of a comprehensive BMD system.[15] The test of June 10,

1984, of a ground-based MHV in a BMD mode clearly demonstrates the reality of this relationship, for the target could have been a dummy satellite instead of a dummy warhead.

The ASAT loophole in the ABM Treaty also implies that there would be little sense in pursuing ASAT arms control if one is planning to deploy a space-based BMD system. As it is, the ABM Treaty is a roadblock to the would-be builder of such a system. Furthermore, the owner of a space-based BMD system will need ASATs to defend his own orbiting battle platforms and space-based surveillance instruments and to attack those of his adversary.

The ABM Treaty is based on the recognition that antimissile defense of the territory of one nation will trigger a buildup of offensive missiles of the other. The portion of this book devoted to space-based BMD argues that this insight remains as valid today as in 1972. No matter what its true purpose may be, ASAT activity will be viewed as a stalking horse for a BMD program. As a result, the deployment of ASATs could eventually trigger the buildup of offensive missiles, even if the space-based BMD program never leaves the laboratory.

13:

THE ASAT THREAT WITH AND WITHOUT A TREATY

The value of a ban on ASAT space tests is best measured by looking ahead to the variety of ASAT threats that can be expected in the next five to ten years if there are no further restraints on weapons competition in outer space. In that period the total number of American satellites will increase to about a hundred, with approximately one-third of these in low earth orbits, about one-fifth in semi-synchronous orbits, about one-third in geosynchronous orbits, with the remainder in highly elliptical orbits.

If the Soviets are free to continue ASAT development, we may anticipate the following course of space weapons competition. A first, conservative Soviet move might be to improve their interceptor so that it could reach higher altitudes, and also to defeat potential U.S. satellite defense measures, such as radar jammers, decoys, and evasion. Tests of the current Soviet interceptor up to geosynchronous orbits might be feasible within relatively few years, if the Soviets set themselves to it. This would mean matching the interceptor to a new booster, such as the liquid-fueled PROTON or A-2 rockets used to orbit the Salyut and Soyuz space vehicles. The whole system would require testing against space targets to confirm that it worked, however, and the long launch preparations needed for such massive boosters would make this a very cumbersome ASAT.

Alternatively, the Soviets could pursue a more promising ASAT development program along one or more of at least three paths: a more agile miniature ASAT interceptor, like the one the United States is developing, that could reach all altitudes with smaller boosters; a more exotic orbiting laser ASAT; or space mines. A space mine is a small satellite that carries an explosive charge and is placed in an orbit to follow closely its potential target. It could then be commanded instantly to destroy the satellite it has accompanied for weeks or months. Space mines are difficult to detect and difficult to defeat. Unless negotiated restrictions are placed on ASATs, it is very likely that space mines will soon pose a critical threat to satellite systems in conventional war or at the outbreak of nuclear war.

Since the president's Star Wars speech, debate over the feasibility and cost of space-based lasers has reached a fever pitch, but there is no question that both sides are vigorously developing them. According to Air Force chief of research and development General Kelley Burke, the Soviets are believed capable of launching a laser ASAT of limited effectiveness within five years, and a more effective system may be ready for launch in the 1990s. In keeping with their accustomed practice, the Soviets may well develop and deploy a mix of ASAT weapons, each posing a different threat to U.S. satellites: improved ground-based interceptors and lasers for lower orbit attacks, space-based lasers for higher orbits, and space mines for attacks at all altitudes. Along the way, the number of launch sites would be increased, inventories of ready-to-fire ASAT weapons would multiply, and all U.S. satellites would become progressively more vulnerable to attack.

The United States has already mapped out its initial moves in this competition. In the beginning, the U.S. Air Force will incorporate defenses on satellites, and deploy the sophisticated F-15 ASAT MHV interceptor. Ground- and air-based lasers under active development by the Defense Advanced Research Projects Agency in the Pentagon will provide additional ASAT capability against low-orbit satellites while helping to solve technical problems in the development of space-based lasers. A "defensive" space-based laser weapon—an ASAT deployed to attack Soviet ASATs—could be the next step. If the vision of Star Wars achieves any reality, these developments will accelerate, and the resulting scene might recall the battleship competitions of an earlier era, where each side strove for the competitive edge of just a bit more firepower, longer range, thicker armor, and larger fleets.

Under such unrestrained ASAT competition, the advantage will almost certainly go to the offense. A duel between a sophisticated ASAT weapon devised for the sole task of killing and a satellite built for other purposes and only incidentally equipped to defend itself will always be a mismatch. Moreover, U.S. satellites are designed for lifetimes of five to ten years, so the defenses they carry with them into space on the day of launch stand a good chance of being nullified in a rapidly changing ASAT environment. Soviet satellites have much shorter lifetimes, are therefore more frequently replaced, and could be more readily modified to counter fresh U.S. ASAT developments.

Large-scale deployment of ASATs could have very serious implications for crisis stability and reduce the chance for averting catastrophic escalation of a nuclear conflict. Although the shape and form of these dangers cannot be foreseen with certainty, the overall trends are clear enough.

The current generation of ASATs, the U.S. F-15 and the Soviet co-orbital interceptor, can attack only satellites in low orbits. Nevertheless, satellites in such orbits provide military commanders with invaluable intelligence concerning the status and disposition of enemy forces. As early as 1968, Soviet preparations for the invasion of Czechoslovakia were observed by U.S. intelligence with the help of satellites. Today, digital images in the visible and infrared can be transmitted to ground stations at extremely high speed. The speed of transmission of such images, as well as their quality, is continually improving. In addition, a wide range of radio signals can be intercepted and analyzed by satellites and their ground stations.

In the foreseeable future, satellites carrying radars will provide all-weather, night-and-day information concerning the movement of objects as small as tanks. If a prompt, comprehensive low-altitude ASAT capability exists, the temptation to destroy this intelligence-gathering system in a crisis or at the outset of actual conflict could prove to be irresistible, especially if one knows that the opponent could also pounce on one's own satellites at any moment. Consequently, ASAT attacks accompanying the start of what might otherwise have been a skirmish could create a major conflagration. Another possibility is that a crisis that might have been defused by diplomacy could come undone because of preemptive ASAT attacks. In short, if both sides have potent low-altitude ASAT capabilities (and it is inconceivable that only one side would be able to retain such a capability for long), crises and skirmishes that might otherwise have been contained could lead to large-scale conventional conflict. Since it is widely acknowledged that the most likely route to nuclear war is via such a conflict, one should recognize that even the current generation of ASATs carry with them the seeds for nuclear war.

If sophisticated ASATs capable of prompt attack against geosynchronous satellites come into operation, the implications for crisis stability are graver still. For both sides would then have deep concerns that the central nervous system of their strategic forces could be surgically eradicated. Such vulnerability of the strategic command and control system is a likely by-product of any attempt to deploy space-based BMD weapons, even if such weapons never attain the capacity to carry out their defensive mission.

In addition to these risks, the intensive testing that would precede large-scale ASAT deployments—indeed, the mere presence of ASATs—would create further hazards. Because attacks on satellites could be an opening step in war, even inadvertent events in space may be mistaken as a signal that war has begun. The sheer multiplicity of ASATs would also raise the likelihood of such an accidental event, which in fact has happened in the past. In 1975, for example, there was concern that U.S. early-warning satellites had been attacked by Soviet infrared lasers. It was later established that these satellites had merely observed infrared radiation from a Soviet natural gas pipeline fire.

In an unrestrained ASAT competition, protecting

American satellites through hardening, maneuvering, deception, and the like, against ever more sophisticated and nimble Soviet ASATs, will become infeasible. Exotic laser ASATs may well prove unworkable in the near future, but the Soviets would still be free to duplicate the U.S. miniature ASAT interceptor and threaten American satellites at all altitudes. Five to ten years from now, after successive rounds of unrestrained competition, the security of U.S. satellites, and thereby of the United States, will have been seriously impaired, despite greatly increased expenditures. In sum, the contrast between a future with ASAT arms control and one without is stark.

Were a satisfactory ASAT arms control agreement in force, the future would look quite different. As matters stand now, only a fraction of U.S. satellites are exposed to the rudimentary Soviet ASAT system. Under a general ban on tests of ASAT systems in space, Soviet efforts to improve their current interceptor or to devise a new one should be blunted. Tests or use of lasers or high-powered transmitters to damage satellite sensors or to burn out satellite receivers would be banned.

An initial ban on ASAT tests could soon be augmented by a wider agreement to dismantle ASATs. Until such time as a comprehensive ban on possession of an ASAT system could be negotiated, however, there would still be a limited Soviet ASAT threat to those U.S. satellites within reach of the current Soviet interceptor. It would be doing arms control a disservice to claim that ASAT arms control alone could protect all space assets, just as extravagant claims that acquriing ASAT weapons will solve all our problems are equally mistaken. What ASAT limitations could do is to make the task of protecting satellites less difficult and more reliable and thus enhance confidence in the survival of satellites vital to U.S. security. ASAT arms control, then, serves American security interests by being an indispensable adjunct to, not a replacement for, U.S. programs to diversify its satellite functions and harden its satellites against attacks.

Under a general ban on space tests of ASATs, the United States would have to forgo further tests in space of the ASAT interceptor it is now developing. If an ASAT accord were reached promptly, or if the United States offered to improve the prospects for successful negotiations by agreeing to the voluntary test moratorium first proposed by the late Soviet leader Yuri Andropov, the outcome might be that the United States would have little test experience with its ASAT in space, while the Soviets would have conducted some twenty tests over the past fifteen years. But there are compensations that must be weighed. The Soviet's ASAT test program has not been a great success. The United States has already accumulated significant test and engineering experience, so it would not be left with a blank slate. Furthermore, unless the United States closes off further ASAT testing soon, it risks exposing all its vital satellites to possible improvements in the Soviet ASAT system, improvements that might require years of American effort and billions of dollars to offset, if in fact they could be offset at all.

In agreeing not to use ASATs, the United States would also forgo one of the stated purposes of buying its ASAT system: attacking Soviet satellites that can be used to target U.S. military forces. The principal satellites of concern are the Soviet radar ocean reconnaissance satellites (RORSATs) and electronic ocean reconnaissance satellites (EORSATs) that can locate ships at sea. It is important to assess whether this limitation would significantly compromise American security. In doing so, however, one must not forget that we too have satellites that have an important role in monitoring and targeting Soviet forces; we cannot expect to attain and maintain a monopoly on ASATs that can destroy satellites posing a threat to military forces. Such a balanced assessment was made in a statement of May 2, 1984, to the House Foreign Affairs Committee by Admiral Noel Gayler (USN, Ret.), who has served both as commander in chief of all U.S. forces in the Pacific and as the director of the National Security Agency.

Admiral Gayler pointed out that naval vessels emit and receive a wide variety of electronic signals to navigate; to communicate with each other, with aircraft, and with shore; and to scan the sea and sky to detect potential attackers. These signals range from high-powered radar to many distinct radio channels, and they can be intercepted by Soviet ground, sea and air stations in addition to the Soviet EORSAT satellites. Elimination of the EORSATs by U.S. ASATs would not remove the risk that Soviet electronic intelligence could locate, identify, and track our ships. To mitigate this danger, the Navy attempts, in exercises, to operate in electronic silence, but, Admiral Gayler declared, his experience as a commander of aircraft carriers and large naval formations showed that such silence cannot be maintained for long without a serious loss of combat effectiveness. He observed that the way out of this danger is well known, but it is totally dependent on the availability of friendly satellites to provide accurate navigation data from the Global Positioning System, ocean surveillance to reduce reliance on shipboard radar, and above all, high data-rate line-of-sight communications from ship to satellite, which is essentially impossible to intercept. As for the Soviet radar satellites (RORSATs), they can be spoofed by deployment of fake targets. The treaty we propose in this book permits nondestructive jamming, which is a highly effective countermeasure against the satellite's relatively weak radar. These considerations demonstrate that the vital task of keeping open the sea lanes that link the American oceanic alliance would be greatly facilitated if U.S. military space systems were not at risk. It is therefore in the U.S. Navy's interest to prevent developments that would threaten our satellites—most prominently, an ASAT rivalry with the Soviet Union.

Analogous conclusions apply to other U.S. forces. Any force designed to operate on the periphery of the Soviet Union, where U.S. alliance obligations are, must be equipped with an array of countermeasures and defenses against Soviet surveillance from all quarters, not only from space. Furthermore, if the Soviets were to initiate hostilities, they would have gathered and transmitted the satellite information needed to target U.S. forces *before* they struck. The United States would be unlikely to shoot down Soviet satellites preemptively on *suspicion* of Soviet intentions; doing so would certainly provoke hostilities. And for some time after hostilities broke out, the Soviets might also be able to launch new satellites to replace those destroyed by a U.S. ASAT; American military forces would again have to be prepared to fend for themselves in the face of threatening Soviet satellites.

Finally, U.S. military forces (with the exception of submarines) cannot count indefinitely upon concealment for their survival. They must be prepared sooner or later to withstand the brunt of Soviet forces. A U.S. ASAT system cannot protect an aircraft carrier once it is discovered by shooting down Soviet antiship missiles or by intercepting torpedoes. It is worth noting in this regard that the U.S. ASAT program diverts resources and funds from other defense programs vital to our forces. According the the General Accounting Office, the U.S. ASAT program is already slated to cost $3.6 billion and could well rise to "tens of billions." Even at $3.6 billion, the "opportunity cost" of the ASAT system already equals one Nimitz-class nuclear-powered aircraft carrier. Where such trade-offs are involved, an ASAT system is not an incidental option, but potentially a major drain upon overall U.S. military preparedness.

The most important concern for the United States is to ensure that its satellites can carry out their tasks even in crisis or conflict. Using an ASAT to shoot down Soviet satellites would not protect or restore U.S. satellites. It is occasionally argued that the American ASAT can deter Soviet ASAT attacks by the threat of a tit-for-tat response. Given America's greater dependence upon satellites and the greater cost of individual U.S. satellites, such a tit-for-tat exchange would most likely only make the situation worse for the United States. The best "deterrent" to Soviet ASAT attacks is Soviet awareness that U.S. satellite functions are so well diversified and hardened and so well supplemented by non-satellite systems that no attack on satellites could succeed in crippling our overall military capability. An American ASAT system contributes nothing to this "deterrent"; it promises only to divert funds from the countermeasures that would genuinely provide such security.

14:

VERIFICATION AND RESIDUAL RISKS

It has been argued that ASAT arms control poses daunting, perhaps even insuperable, verification problems, more than any other area of arms control. One reason offered for this is that satellites are so few in number and their capabilities so difficult to duplicate with ground-based alternatives that even a few ASAT weapons covertly acquired in violation of an agreement could reward the cheater with significant military advantage in a conflict. It is also argued that any limitations on weapons or space programs comprehensive enough to close off such cheating would necessarily be so stringent they would preclude many civilian uses of outer space. As an illustration, the Soviet Progrez resupply vehicles used in the Salyut program have features in common with ASAT interceptors: they can be launched into the vicinity of an orbiting satellite, maneuvered alongside, and brought into contact. Yet banning or limiting all such maneuvering space vehicles to prevent them from being configured as ASAT weapons would impair not only the Salyut program but the U.S.

Space Shuttle as well. The problems are multiplied if one considers the ASAT potential of other weapons not specifically designed as ASATs, such as ground-based ABM interceptor missiles or nuclear-tipped ICBMs or exotic, directed energy air defenses.

These arguments point to genuine concerns the United States ought to have about the survivability of its satellites. At the same time, they assume that the future is dictated by past errors. In the past, the United States coped with limited budgets and high launching costs (hundreds, even thousands of dollars per kilogram to place objects in orbit) by relying on relatively few long-lived equipment-crammed satellites to perform vital military tasks. Little effort was made to incorporate survivability measures or to diversify functions. Because of their design and budgeting constraints, U.S. satellites are vulnerable to even primitive ASAT weapons.

But with or without ASAT arms control, the United States cannot go on like this. Nor does it intend to. A presidential directive in May 1978 ordered that all future U.S. military satellites be equipped with survivability measures and devices for detecting ASAT attacks. Some satellites probably cannot be protected from attacks at any affordable cost (e.g., large and fragile low-orbit satellites); and some attacks may work against almost any satellite (e.g., nuclear warheads detonated near a satellite). The best approach to reducing the risk is to move to a larger number of simpler, easily replaced satellites that are much more readily protected by decoys. Yet even this technique will succeed only if the Soviets are stopped from developing a cheap, nimble ASAT system capable of promptly attacking great numbers of satellites. It is precisely this sort of development that an ASAT arms control agreement should prevent.

There are several verification tasks that must be tackled under a general ban on ASAT weapons tests and use. The United States would have to confirm that the existing Soviet ASAT interceptor was not being tested in space; that no new ASAT weapons were being devised and tested in space or against space targets, including such exotic new ASATs as ground- or air-based lasers that could be aimed at low-orbit satellites; that weapons originally designed and deployed for other missions were not being tested in an ASAT mode; and that non-weapon space vehicles and programs were not posing significant ASAT threats.

The United States already has a diverse array of intelligence and space surveillance facilities for keeping track of Soviet activities, and this array is being expanded. NORAD, the North American Aerospace Defense Command, maintains a Space Object Catalogue that is constantly updated to record the identity and current orbits of all space objects (several thousand in all, of which several hundred are active or defunct satellites). NORAD's space tracking radar network has recently been upgraded to provide greater tracking accuracy, and gaps in the network have been closed by installing and improving radars in the Pacific. The GEODSS (Ground-based Electro-Optical Deep Space Surveillance) system, when completed in 1987, will augment ground radars and provide precise, highly detailed optical and orbital data on man-made objects approximately 4,800 kilometers from earth and beyond. Upgraded radars in the United States, Turkey, and Kwajalein will provide additional tracking of objects in geosynchronous orbits.

Other electronic and optical sensors deployed around and over the Soviet Union add to U.S. ability to detect and classify Soviet missile and space launches. The potential for monitoring activities *in* outer space *from* space must also be considered. The recent demonstration of what is possible in inspecting damaged and missing thermal tiles on the first Space Shuttle flight in April 1981 hints at what might be routinely feasible. Critiques of space verification capabilities tend to match only *current* monitoring capacities against *future* conceivable but nonexistent ASAT weapons, and not surprisingly, these assessments come to pessimistic conclusions. More imaginative evaluations should consider what we could now do but have not funded, as well as potential innovations in monitoring capabilities. In particular, under a treaty-restricted regime it would become worthwhile to make specialized observation systems to monitor the infrared emission from Soviet satellites in order to determine whether they were being heated by ground-based or airborne lasers, to provide close-in photographs of maneuverable space objects, and the like.

The effectiveness of all the monitoring facilities would be enhanced under an arms control agreement by provisions—such as those included in prior accords —prohibiting both interference with national technical means of verification and deliberate concealment that impedes verification. Since the Soviets have already agreed in principle that arms control accords may include cooperative measures contributing to the effectiveness of verification by national technical means (in the SALT II Joint Statement of Principles), these too should be exploited to improve confidence in verification.

The United States already has fifteen years monitoring experience with tests of the current Soviet ASAT interceptor (see Table 5 in Chapter 10), so clandestine tests of the existing Soviet ASAT would be very difficult at best. The only tests that would stand a reasonable chance of evading detection would have to attack a point in space, leave the interceptor intact, and avoid the deft approach maneuvers characteristic of ASAT activity. Such constrained tests would be of very limited value. They could possibly confirm that the ASAT with the active radar homer performs as in the past test series. Perhaps they could even demonstrate that improvements have made the device more reliable. But the Soviets could not rely on such tests to evaluate more sophisticated and powerful homing techniques or approach tactics because a point in space, even if moved by computer, is not a maneuvering source of infrared radiation.

Conceivably the Soviets might try to test their current ASAT covertly in some radically different manner that expanded its capabilities—for example, on a new booster capable of interception significantly higher than its present ceiling. This would not be a "nimble" threat, even in the unlikely event that cheating succeeded. The booster required to loft the Soviet's bulky ASAT up to geosynchronous altitudes would have to be comparable with the large U.S. Saturn 1B or the Soviet PROTON booster, massive rockets with long preparation times, whose launches would be unmistakable.

More likely, if the Soviets hoped to expand their ASAT capability covertly, they would attempt an entirely new weapon, such as a miniature homing ASAT, a more exotic laser ASAT, or space mines. Until such time as ASATs are banned altogether, neither side would be violating the limitations if they devised such systems on the ground; they would be banned from testing them in space or against space objects.

The technological challenges in building an effective space-based laser ASAT are formidable, however, even if unrestricted testing in space were permitted, and doing it all covertly would certainly be a protracted, highly risky task. To prevent the Soviets from testing ASATs in space under the pretense of developing, for instance, a space-based laser antiaircraft defense system, a treaty should also ban space weapons for damaging or destroying objects in the atmosphere or on the ground. This prohibition would also reinforce existing limitations on space weapons in the 1967 Outer Space Treaty and the 1972 ABM Treaty.

Space-based lasers with a large kill range are discussed at length in the BMD portion of this book. Due to their obvious external characteristics and serious technical hurdles, clandestine development of such lasers to the stage of an operational weapon system would be a most unproductive undertaking. Ground-based lasers could probably be developed secretly, but their ASAT potential is far from obvious. If the intended target is a low-orbit satellite, the laser weapon suffers from the fundamental disadvantages of any ground-launched ASAT in that it is usually not in a suitable position for any given target. A laser would have the additional handicap of requiring a clear sky. If the laser is intended for attack on geosynchronous satellites, the density fluctuations in the atmosphere would create a serious problem. These ever-present fluctuations produce a very significant outward flaring of the laser beam. As a result, the beam forms an ineffectually diffuse spot at geosynchronous altitude. A ground-based laser, as a component of a BMD system, could meet this problem using cooperative equipment on a geosynchronous relay mirror that provides a means of compensating the distortion of the laser beam. But such measures are hardly available when the geosynchronous device is hostile and to be destroyed. So the owner of the clandestine ground-based laser ASAT is likely to need some space-based components to create an effective system, and that makes it very difficult to evade detection by verification systems.

Whether Soviet technology is sufficiently far advanced to make a miniature homing ASAT feasible in the near future is not clear. In all the new ASATs, however, very high accuracies in homing or aiming would be necessary, and such accuracies would be difficult to confirm without actual tests against space targets. Such tests can leave a host of telltale signs: launch of the ASAT itself; a large flow of data that the Soviets would have to transmit from the test vehicles; damage to the target that causes it to fragment or tumble[16]; intense heating that can be detected by infrared sensors; and displacement of the target's orbit. While the Soviets were pressing ahead with such innovations, there would of course be a parallel expansion and evolution of U.S. monitoring facilities, which would further facilitate detection of cheating.

Space mines placed in orbit near targets and detonated only when conflict begins present another verification problem. They seem ingeniously simple. The technology could perhaps be fairly primitive, and if the only tests required were triggering the explosive upon command, they could be amply tested on earth. Nevertheless, if covertly deployed, they might give themselves away or pose only a manageable threat. The orbital paths of satellites are not necessarily stable, especially those of satellites in lower orbits that are subject to atmospheric drag or that maneuver to perform their missions. Space mines dogging along behind such maneuvering satellites would be bound to raise suspicions. And the mine ceases to be such a simple device if it must be equipped with homing and maneuvering capabilities so that it is able to track its potential target or to close in rapidly on command. At geosynchronous altitudes, where all orbits are more stable, a space mine skulking near its target could still arouse suspicions, since all legitimate satellites are supposed to be registered (under the 1975 Convention on Registration of Objects Launched into Outer Space) and are to maintain minimum separation distances in geosynchronous orbits. Again, a space mine becomes a complex device if it must pretend to be something benign when far away from its target to avoid suspicions but can swiftly seek its target upon command.

When it comes to verifying that non-ASAT weapons are not being put to ASAT purposes, long U.S. experience at monitoring the characteristic patterns of Soviet ICBM and ABM tests would make it risky for the Soviets to test these weapons in an ASAT mode. Even in the absence of tests, such weapons would still have to be taken into account as an ASAT threat, since the great kill-distance of nuclear explosions in space could compensate for deficiencies in guidance systems or test experience. But it is also true that present ABM interceptors can reach satellites only in the lowest orbits, and any nuclear explosion in space carries a grave risk of escalation, of damage to "friendly" satellites as well as the target, and of uncertain, although possibly dramatic, EMP effects upon other military and civilian systems on earth. So while such residual ASAT threats are less awesome than what unrestricted ASAT competition would produce, they would persist, even if the ability to verify a test ban were perfect. They call for continuing vigorous satellite survivability programs as an adjunct to ASAT arms control.

Some non-weapon space vehicles may also have inherent ASAT capability—resupply vehicles that can home in on other satellites, for example—and the United States would want to verify that such vehicles were not being tested in an ASAT mode. The overlap of non-weapon space technology with ASAT missions should not be exaggerated, however. The continuing high cost of launching anything into space will certainly force designers to concentrate on the requirements of space vehicles' specific non-weapon missions, and the result is not likely to be a very agile or capable ASAT. The Soviet's Progrez resupply vehicle, for instance, is obviously designed to deliver the maximum amount of provisions in few trips. Its takeoff weight, fully loaded, is perhaps three times that of the Soviet's own bulky ASAT, and it requires an enormous booster just to reach altitudes of a few hundred miles. Such jury-rigged ASATs are not very good foundations for a weapons system to "sweep the skies." Indeed, any clandestine ASAT that exploits large maneuvering spacecraft is intrinsically a slow interceptor not suitable for attacking a set of satellites at widely separated positions in a short span of time. It is very questionable whether such a ponderous ASAT capability has any significant military value.

Nevertheless, an ASAT arms control agreement could incorporate collateral constraints on the characteristics and use of non-weapon space technologies. These constraints might include, for instance, limits upon speed of approach in rendezvous maneuvers, or upon power/aperture characteristics of lasers in space. It would, however, be premature to propose a long list of such constraints right now. The treaty we propose would accommodate such collateral constraints in several ways. Cases that the parties find of immediate concern could be addressed in treaty negotiations and incorporated as additional articles or perhaps as cooperative measures in test or space-use procedures that aid verification. Limits on future cases involving new technologies could best be addressed on a case-by-case basis in the Standing Consultative Commission, as the specific dimensions of problems and remedies become clear. This approach would raise our confidence that such space vehicles were not being readied as ASATs, while minimizing the impact upon non-weapon space exploration.

A final verification concern is that of breakout—the possibility that the Soviet Union could assemble a significant ASAT capability by abruptly abrogating the treaty and running a quick set of space tests. At issue here is how close to operational status an ASAT weapon could be brought if it were assembled and tested only on the ground or covertly in space as dismantled components (e.g., testing homing sensors for ASAT interceptors on some ostensibly non-weapon space mission). Remarkable inconsistencies occasionally crop up in arguments on this matter. On the one hand, it is claimed that the Soviets could readily concoct an ASAT system even though space tests were banned; on the other, it is asserted that the United States could not accept a ban on testing because then it would be unable to confirm that its own ASAT system works. A more balanced viewpoint is in order here.

The United States has already conducted enough tests of its own ASAT interceptor to be ready for tests against targets in space, so even if a moratorium on tests were agreed to now, the United States would not be without experience. Indeed, the June 1984 MHV test was against a target in space. If the ASAT accord banned tests but allowed both sides to keep their present ASAT weapons, then clearly both would have some breakout potential. Though the challenge posed by the existing Soviet ASAT is much more tractable than what unrestrained ASAT competition would bring, this breakout potential would be of some concern to the United States. A combination of reasonable survivability measures and eroding Soviet confidence in their ASAT in the absence of tests, however, would dampen such concerns.

Breakout using an entirely new ASAT weapon that had been tested only on the ground or covertly in space would be quite risky, technically and politically. In ASAT weapons, as in modern weaponry generally, capability and complexity are linked: the more capable a weapon is in coping with a variety of combat requirements, the more complicated it is likely to be and the more in need of tests that simulate actual engagements. Soviet attempts to conduct realistic full-system ASAT tests in space covertly would confront the whole battery of U.S. intelligence sensors. On the other hand, breaking the ASAT system down into component parts for covert testing, in order to minimize the chance of detection, entails a real risk that the whole system will not work as well operationally as the parts. The Soviets have clearly experienced gaps between plans and performance in space and weapon systems, and even catastrophic shortcomings. Without tests, the Soviets could not confidently predict how soon a new device could be made to work after breakout—if at all. An ASAT test ban could serve American interests by exploiting Soviet uncertainties and fear of detection while leaving the United States free to complicate the Soviets' breakout task through a variety of satellite defensive measures.

In sum, there is no obvious reason why an arms control agreement banning space tests and use of ASAT weapons could not be adequately verifiable. There may be some areas of uncertainty, but they are not so great as to permit the Soviets to pose a significant unanticipated threat to U.S. security if we take prudent steps toward improving intelligence capabilities and diversifying and protecting vital satellite functions.

15:

THE ADMINISTRATION'S ASAT POLICY

On a number of occasions in 1982 and 1983, committees of Congress tried without success to elicit statements from senior officials of the Reagan administration as to the president's ASAT arms control policy. Following considerable activity in both the House and the Senate, the Defense Appropriations Act for Fiscal Year 1984 was passed with a provision that some $19 million in ASAT funding could not be spent unless the president provided a report by March 31, 1984, describing the "specific steps [he] contemplates undertaking . . . to seek a verifiable agreement with the Soviet Union to ban or strictly limit existing and future ASAT systems."

The administration complied with this provision on the deadline day with a report entitled "U.S. Policy on ASAT Arms Control." This document finally clarified the administration's position with the unambiguous conclusion that "no arrangements or agreements beyond those already governing military activities in outer space have been found to date that are judged to be in the overall interest of the United States and its allies," and that it would not "be productive to engage in formal international negotiations."

The considerations the report cites in support of this conclusion fall into several distinct categories. Some bear no discernible relationship to ASAT arms control, others could be addressed only in actual negotiations, while a few are legitimate concerns that must be settled by the government prior to negotiation. Unfortunately, the report does not separate its case into these categories. Above all, it does not draw up a balance sheet that weighs the advantages against the disadvantages of the unrestrained ASAT competition that it advocates, as compared with the treaty-constrained regime that it discards. We will, below, evaluate the president's report with the aid of our own balance sheet.

The report cites concerns that have nothing to do with ASAT arms control, or for that matter with any form of arms control. In particular, it points out that existing strategic nuclear weapons, such as ICBMs and SLBMs, could be used to attack satellites and that ASAT arms control would not "provide for survivability" of vulnerable ground-support facilities. But that has nothing to do with arms control. Acts of war can be averted only by remaining at peace.

A number of points in the report can be addressed only in negotiation. The report questions the motives behind various Soviet ASAT arms control initiatives, especially the offer of a moratorium on ASAT flight tests, and suggests that these are primarily designed to curtail the U.S. ASAT program. ASAT development and negotiations were originally intended to be two facets of a single policy, whose primary goal was a ban on ASAT weapons, and ASAT deployment was to proceed only if negotiations failed. So one could regard the Soviet proposal as a sign that the U.S. ASAT program is now playing its originally intended role as a bargaining chip. But that is a question that can be truly answered only by engaging in negotiations. In the absence of bilateral talks, however, ASATs will join the long list of former bargaining chips that now form significant portions of today's strategic arsenals.

The president's report criticizes the Soviet 1983 draft treaty by pointing to a variety of shortcomings. One of these is well taken and was already mentioned in Chapter 11. But this criticism does not disqualify the Soviet 1983 draft as a valid point of departure for serious negotiations.

Another category of issues that is not germane at this juncture concerns definitions of what constitutes an ASAT weapon and whether highly sensitive information would have to be divulged in setting up the cooperative measures that would facilitate verification. Surely these points, too, important though they may be, can be addressed only in negotiations.

Some questions should be settled before negotiations begin, however. A few of these are discussed in the March 1984 report. The most fundamental of these is whether the United States needs ASATs in view of the threat posed by Soviet military satellites and ASATS. As we have said, the United States is more dependent on satellites than the Soviet Union and as a result it is to America's net disadvantage if both nations' satellites are at risk. The threat posed to the U.S. Navy by Soviet reconnaissance satellites cannot be eliminated by destroying those satellites. Indeed, the Navy's security would be best served if it were to counter that threat by jamming and spoofing and by adopting interception-proof communications via satellites.* The capacity to destroy military satellites could be irresistibly seductive on the eve of hostilities, despite the obvious risk of escalation, so a prompt and comprehensive ASAT capability could destabilize a crisis or low-level conflict. As for the current Soviet ASAT, the president's report does not emphasize this Soviet capability in advocating the administration's position.

The administration's report ignores or glosses over crucial facts. The contention that the United States must have ASATs to deter attacks on our satellites and to protect our military forces is presented on a stage whose set does not depict the world as it really is. There is no mention of our greater reliance on military space systems, a fact that casts doubt on the report's assertion that "a U.S. capability to destroy satellites clearly responds to the need to deter such Soviet attacks on U.S. satellites," and that "a U.S. ASAT capability would contribute to deterrence of conventional conflict." While the report repeatedly states that the United States must have a capability to threaten Soviet satellites that enhance the effectiveness of Soviet forces, no mention is made of the benefit to the United States in protecting U.S. satellites that play an analogous role. Finally, while the report states that "we consider the [Soviet ASAT system] operational" and points to the Soviet test program and the participation of the ASAT

*Vice Admiral Gordon Nagler, who is in charge of the Navy's command and control, has also contested the claim that Soviet ocean reconnaissance satellites could target U.S. aircraft carriers. That electronic countermeasures can foil Soviet ocean reconnaissance satellites has been stated by Admiral Gayler and was recently confirmed by Robert W. Buchheim, formerly chief scientist to the Air Force; see R. Jeffrey Smith, *Science,* May 18, 1984, p. 694.

in the strategic exercise of June 1982, it fails to mention the USSR's test record and the fact that the ASAT failed in the strategic exercise.

In sum, the administration report fails to demonstrate that an ASAT capability would, on balance, serve U.S. national security interests.

The report emphasizes that America, relying on a relatively small number of satellites, might be vulnerable to even small-scale cheating should there be an ASAT treaty. But it acknowledges that this threat, and whatever threat the current Soviet ASAT poses, could be countered by such protective measures as orbiting spare satellites and launching satellites on demand. The report correctly points out that "this philosophy runs counter to current trends of developing space systems of greater sophistication and longer expected mission life time," and that "this option would require considerable investment, not now envisioned, in boosters, spacecraft production, launch facilities and ground support." What the report fails to say is that the administration cannot opt for unconstrained ASAT competition and at the same time expect to to have the luxury of choosing a space deployment philosophy to its liking. The Soviet Union must be expected to field ASATs that will force the United States to adopt protective measures and incur expenses that are "not now envisioned."

The central point in the report is the administration's contention that "no way has yet been found to design a comprehensive ASAT test ban" that can be adequately verified by national technical means. Unfortunately, the report does not define what it means by "comprehensive," but it gives the distinct impression that all activities that have any conceivable ASAT potential are to be covered by the test ban. If that is the case, then it is surely true that verification is either impossible or impractical. In describing the ASAT threat in this way, the administration has abandoned its responsibility to find treaty language that is properly matched to U.S. surveillance technology and, more important, that enhances the security of our satellites.

In claiming that the risk of undetected ASAT tests is so grave that it should preclude negotiation, the administration is in effect taking the position of a society that decides it will not hire police or install traffic signals to control automobile travel because they would not eradicate accidents or car theft, and suggests instead that its citizens drive tanks. Common sense tells us that such a Draconian solution to the traffic problem is both costly and paranoid. And the metaphor is not so far-fetched, because after a period of intense ASAT competition military satellites will bear a relation to today's satellites analogous to that between tanks and automobiles.

The administration's view of the ASAT verification problem is not shared by many of the nation's most prominent experts. Consider the observation of Leslie Dirks, who retired in 1982 after six years as the CIA's deputy director for research and technology:

I'm quite confident that testing things surreptitiously in space is a hard thing to do, and that the U.S. has a very robust detection capability in this area. It would be difficult to guarantee absolutely that no testing was going on. But I hope one would take a liberal view of the verification problems and be prepared to take a few risks, because there are clearly strong U.S. interests in a treaty that would deter continued testing of the Soviet ASAT or prevent the development of a better Soviet system.[17]

Dirks emphasizes that the issue is not whether the Soviets can test components but whether they can test the entire system: "I spent about twenty years engaging the Soviets on this issue, and I know that the Soviet military would be very unwilling to depend on a system that had not been fully tested."*

The verification of tests of laser ASATs are similarly assessed by Dr. Michael May, associate director of the Lawrence Livermore Laboratory and a member of the scientific panel that reviewed the report of the Fletcher Commission. May expresses the view that under appropriate circumstances tests of ground- and air-based lasers could escape detection, but that the useful range of such weapons would be limited, while a significant ASAT threat would require "the installation of a high-powered laser system [that] would be detectable."

Chapter 14 described the technical facilities now available to monitor Soviet space activities, and technologies that could be developed specifically for the purpose of verification. There has been a recent development that bears on the issue of verification, however, which deserves a brief discussion.

In testimony on March 1, 1984, before the House Armed Services Committee, Dr. Richard DeLauer made a revealing comment about the Star Wars initiative that is relevant to ASAT verification. His comment also reflects the opinion of the Defensive Technology Study headed by James C. Fletcher. Space-based BMD

---

*Precisely the same point was made to the House Foreign Affairs Committee on May 2, 1982, by Ambassador Robert W. Buchheim, who headed the U.S. team on the SALT Standing Consultative Commission and led the ASAT negotiations in the Carter Administration.

will require a space "surveillance, acquisition, tracking, and kill assessment" system (called SATKA) that can track the thousands of "objects designated as reentry vehicles and other objects that may be confusing to later tiers" of the missile defense. To that end, the Defense Department will explore new airborne infrared sensors, new radar imaging techniques, as well as "ladar," which is similar to radar, but uses laser beams to attain more refined resolution. "Each credible object," stated the Fletcher panel, "must be accounted for [by SATKA] in a birth-to-death track, even if the price is many decoy false alarms. Interceptor vehicles of [our] defense must be also tracked." This system, according to DeLauer, "must operate reliably even in the presence of disturbances caused by nuclear weapons effects or direct enemy attack."

If the administration believes that a space surveillance system of such prodigious capability can be built, it should recognize that a highly stripped-down version of SATKA, which would not have to withstand any form of attack or perform a myriad of tasks in a matter of minutes, could confidently monitor suspicious events to ascertain whether they are clandestine ASAT tests.

A final point concerning the verification issue is that the report fails to distinguish between ASAT technologies that could carry out simultaneous and prompt attacks on a whole class of satellites and slow-approach systems, such as maneuvering spacecraft, which could not attack a widely dispersed set of satellites without being detected. This distinction is emphasized by Walter Slocombe, deputy under secretary of defense for policy in the Carter administration, who explains that "only a high-confidence, high-precision ASAT system would suffice" in a crisis, and that "jury-rigged systems are clearly inadequate."[18] ASATs that satisfy these demanding requirements must be dedicated weapons that have undergone extensive tests in space and are therefore verifiable. The systems that are more likely to be troublesome for verification could have only a limited ASAT capability and are of questionable military significance.

In drawing up a balance sheet of the pros and cons related to ASAT arms control, one must not forget the matter of cost, even though the administration's report completely neglects this issue. If ASATs are being developed and deployed legitimately, a continuous stream of Soviet space activities will have to be monitored and evaluated. Under a test ban, only sporadic events of a suspicious character will require analysis at a more leisurely pace. A far more versatile and quick-response space surveillance system will be required if there is unfettered ASAT activity. By the same token, U.S. satellites will have to be equipped with much more robust protective measures and with a more versatile and elaborate back-up system if tested weapons are ready to attack them than they will if they face only a potential threat from weapons that may have been tested surreptitiously, in which a potential adversary can hardly place great confidence.

The administration's procurement policy for military satellites, its Star Wars initiative, and its entire stance on arms control lead one to suspect that concern about the Soviet's ASAT threat as it exists today, or as it may evolve in an arms control regime, is not a significant factor in the decisions embodied in the report on ASAT arms control. If fear for the security of military satellites were the driving concern, for example, more attention would be paid to satellite protective measures.

Colonel James Reynolds, the retired manager of the Air Force Navstar satellite program, says that the Pentagon has the know-how to defend our satellites against Soviet attack, but prefers to devote its resources to ASAT technology. In paring down the Air Force's FY 1985 budget request, the Defense Department eliminated $18 million for compact computers considered essential to mobile satellite ground stations. As Livermore's Dr. May points out, "making space systems survivable would make ASATs susceptible to negotiation, because it would substantially increase the cost, time and risk involved in an attack, thereby diminishing the prospect and significance of any cheating."[19]

Two factors appear to govern the administration's ASAT policy. The first is a misconception about the proper role of arms control as a component of national defense policy. Monitoring verification is merely a subset of intelligence gathering, but this does not seem to be recognized. Whether we have an ASAT treaty or not, Soviet space activities will have to monitored assiduously. In the words of William Colby, the former CIA director: "We do a pretty good job of verifying today what the Soviets are doing, and a treaty generally makes the process easier. Verification is not an absolute. We are better off if an activity is essentially stopped, even with a possibility for marginal cheating, than we are if the technology is unconstrained."[20] And what is probably a very prominent factor in ASAT policy is not even mentioned in the administration's report: the intimate relationship between ASATs and ballistic missile defense. As we have explained, space-based ballistic missile defense cannot be pursued if there are ASAT constraints. The decision to forgo ASAT negotiations, therefore, is an integral part of the policy that strives for the control of space as a military environment.

As this book goes to press, there are indications that the United States and the Soviet Union may begin negotiations to limit space weapons in September 1984. Unidentified administration officials and some members of Congress have suggested that a treaty that would only ban ASAT activities at high altitudes should be sought by the United States. At first sight, this is an attractive proposal, because neither side can attack satellites in geosynchronous orbits at this time, and geosynchronous ASAT tests would be even easier to monitor than low-altitude tests. Nevertheless, such a restricted ASAT treaty would not be viable if directed energy weapons were developed for BMD purposes. Once such weapons are tested against dummy boosters or warheads at low altitudes, they would have a capability against a geosynchronous target *without* tests at such higher altitudes. The propagation of a directed energy beam (whether it is composed of light at any wavelength, of X rays, or of neutral particles) is completely determined by elementary physics: such a weapon will deliver the same energy per unit area at geosynchronous altitude in 100 seconds as it does at a range of 2,200 miles in one second. Since it could dwell on a satellite indefinitely, such a weapon could be a useful geosynchronous ASAT even if it had failed as a BMD component.

These observations underscore the central theme of this book: only a treaty that forbids all space weapons tests can protect our most valuable military satellites, while an unconstrained pursuit of space-based missile defenses will undermine U.S. security. Such a treaty would still permit research on strategic defenses, and would not close the door forever to the defense-dominated world that all desire. Should unforeseen technical developments occur in a receptive international political climate, renegotiation of existing treaties would hardly pose an insurmountable obstacle.

PART I

Introduction

1. David N. Schwartz, "Past and Present: The Historical Legacy," in Ashton B. Carter and David N. Schwartz, eds., *Ballistic Missile Defense.* Washington, D.C.: The Brookings Institution, 1984; and Herb Lin, "Ballistic Missile Defense: Then and Now," Ithaca: Cornell University Peace Studies Program, October 22, 1983.

2. Richard L. Garwin and Hans A. Bethe, "Anti-Ballistic-Missile Systems," *Scientific American,* March 1968. The first report of the newly formed Union of Concerned Scientists, "ABM ABC," was published in April 1969.

3. Lawrence Freedman, *The Evolution of Nuclear Strategy.* New York: St. Martin's, 1982, especially Chapter 16.

4. John Newhouse, *Cold Dawn: The Story of SALT.* New York: Holt, Rinehart and Winston, 1973; and Gerard Smith, *Doubletalk: The Story of the First Strategic Arms Limitation Talks.* New York: Doubleday, 1980.

5. Desmond Ball, "Targetting for Strategic Deterrence," *Adelphi Papers* No. 185. London: International Institute for Strategic Studies, Summer 1983. See also Peter Prin-

gle and William Arkin, *SIOP: The Secret U.S. Plan for Nuclear War.* New York: W.W. Norton, 1983; and Lawrence Freedman, *The Evolution of Nuclear Strategy,* Chapter 25.

6. Richard Halloran, "Pentagon Draws Up First Strategy for Fighting Long Nuclear War," *New York Times,* May 30, 1982. For a revealing look at the attitudes of Reagan administration officials toward nuclear war, based on interviews, see Robert Scheer, *With Enough Shovels: Reagan, Bush and Nuclear War.* New York: Vintage Books, 1983.

7. Carter and Schwartz, op. cit., p. 436.

8. *Strategic Survey 1981–82.* London: International Institute for Strategic Studies, 1982, p. 15–16.

9. *Report of the President's Commission on Strategic Forces.* Washington, D.C.: April 1984, p. 12.

10. Caspar W. Weinberger, *Annual Report to Congress, Fiscal Year 1985.* Washington, D.C.: Government Printing Office, 1984, p. 193.

11. U.S. Congress, House Committee on Armed Services, Subcommittee on Research and Development, Hearing on the Strategic Defense Initiative, 98th Congress, 2nd session, March 1, 1984.

12. U.S. Congress, House Subcommittees on Research and Development and Investigations, Hearing on H.R. 3073, People Protection Act, 98th Congress, 1st session, November 10, 1983.

13. Ibid.

14. Fred S. Hoffman, study director, *Ballistic Missile Defense and U.S. National Security: Summary Report.* Washington, D.C.: Future Security Strategy Study, October 1983, p. 2.

15. U.S. Congress, House Committee on Armed Services, Subcommittee on Research and Development, Hearing on the Strategic Defense Initiative, 98th Congress, 2nd session, March 1, 1984.

16. *Science,* November 25, 1983, p. 902.

17. *Report of the President's Commission on Strategic Forces.* Washington, D.C., March 21, 1983, p. 8.

18. U.S. Congress, Senate Committee on Foreign Relations, Hearing on Strategic Defense Initiative, 98th Congress, 2nd session, April 25, 1984.

19. Paul B. Stares, "Déjà Vu: The ASAT Debate in Historical Context," *Arms Control Today,* December 1983.

20. *New York Times,* March 19, 1978, p. 8.

21. *Report to the Congress on U.S. Policy on ASAT Arms Control.* Washington, D.C.: White House, March 31, 1984, p. 1.

22. U.S. Congress, House Committee on Appropriations, Subcommittee on Defense, statement of Robert S. Cooper, director, Defense Advanced Research Projects Agency (DARPA), March 23, 1983.

23. *Aviation Week and Space Technology,* July 18, 1983, p. 21.

PART II

Space-Based Missile Defense

1. Furthermore, nuclear weapons could be exploded at high altitudes, and thereby swamp the radars and the infrared and optical sensors on which the defenses rely. Subsequent warheads could then penetrate to a sufficiently low altitude to demolish a soft target.

2. The following statements apply with greatest force to the boost-phase portion of BMD. In midcourse BMD the cost of interceptors, which cannot now be estimated, is of some importance in assessing the effectiveness of the system. This is hardly a critical point, since an effective global BMD appears to require highly efficient boost-phase interception.

3. In testimony before the Senate Armed Services Committee on March 23, 1983, General Lamberson stated that "particle beam technology is currently the least mature of the directed energy technology efforts."

4. For the sake of discussion we thereby grant that the embryonic technology of adaptive optics, in which the shape of the mirror is continuously monitored and corrected by a calibrated source coupled to a feedback mechanism, will eventually lead to the optically perfect (i.e., diffraction limited) large mirrors required.

5. Claims that one can simply "scale up" lasers to higher power output should be treated with caution. High-powered lasers are intrinsically nonlinear systems. As the power is raised, experience has shown that new phenomena often arise and stand in the path to yet higher power levels.

6. This method relies on the fact that the atmospheric fluctuations vary slowly in comparison to the time required

for the downward and upward journeys of the light rays. The technique of phase conjugation is also involved in this scheme. See H. A. Bethe et al., *Scientific American,* October 1984.

7. J. Steinbruner, *Scientific American,* January 1984.

8. According to Under Secretary of Defense Richard DeLauer, the U.S. is superior to the U.S.S.R. in the following technologies relevant to the issue at hand: automated control, computing, electro-optical sensors, guidance and navigation, microelectronics, optics, aerospace propulsion, radar sensors, signal processing, software, stealth (or signal reduction) technology, lightweight high strength materials, and telecommunications. Only in directed energy technology itself, and in nuclear warhead design and fluid dynamics, is the U.S.S.R. rated as equivalent, while it does not lead in any relevant technology (FY 1984 Department of Defense Program for Research, Development, and Acquisition, Statement by Richard DeLauer, 98th Congress, 1st session, 1983, pp. 11–18).

9. Here we have assumed that the pellets are spherical. If these one-ounce pellets were appropriately shaped projectiles, they could penetrate a steel plate perhaps five to ten times thicker. Normally a shaped projectile, such as an artillery shell, maintains its orientation because of air resistance, and because it is spun. In the vacuum of space the projectile will tumble unless the dispenser provides it with sufficient spin. The design of such a dispenser is an engineering problem that is surely simpler than most of the others discussed in this report.

10. There are several prospective weapons that might be suitable for hard-point defense. With special radars and data processing, it appears feasible to use a single stage interceptor (for example an upgraded SPRINT missile)

for RV kill. Alternatively, it is possible to launch a "curtain" of a large number of small projectiles against RVs as they near the ground. In this concept, called Swarm-Jet, at least one of the projectiles would strike the warhead and the combined velocities of the objects would ensure warhead destruction. It is also possible (technically if not politically) to employ shallow underground nuclear detonations to raise a curtain of dust that would stay aloft for an hour or more and prevent RV penetration. Other terminal defenses under study include the use of new types of homing vehicles and airborne weapons. There are, of course, countermeasures available to the attacker. For a period during the start of reentry, the attacker can power decoys and slow reentry vehicles so as to confuse or spoof the discrimination. Reentry vehicles can carry defense radar jammers. And the attacker can employ atmospheric nuclear bursts to black out the radars. Such bursts produce an opaque sphere 2 to 4 km across for tens of seconds, which interrupts tracking and weapons assignment and allows following vehicles a longer run before caught by the radar.

11. *Report of the President's Commission on Strategic Forces,* April 1983, p. 12.

12. Peter Clausen, "Dooming Arms Control," *New York Times,* October 27, 1983, p. A31.

13. See especially the report of the Hoffman panel, *Ballistic Missile Defenses and U.S. National Security: Summary Report,* October 1983.

14. See Desmond Ball, *Can Nuclear War Be Controlled?,* Adelphi Paper 169 (London: International Institute for Strategic Studies, Autumn 1981).

15. Wayne Biddle, "Missile System Change Seen as Threat to Treaty," *New York Times,* April 2, 1984.

16. For extended discussions of the Soviet radar and other arms control treaty compliance issues, see *Arms Control Today,* March–April 1984, and *F.A.S. Public Interest Report,* March 1984.

17. Report of the Secretary of Defense Caspar W. Weinberger to the Congress on the FY 1985 Budget, FY 1986 Authorization Request and FY 1985–89 Defense Programs, February 1, 1984, p. 193.

18. "U.S. and Soviet Defense Plans Threaten ABM Treaty," *National Journal,* January 7, 1984, p. 14.

19. *New York Times,* October 2, 1983.

20. *Washington Post,* April 11, 1984, p. A30; *Christian Science Monitor,* April 12, 1984, p. 1.

21. *Washington Post,* April 4, 1984, p. 18.

22. *Washington Post,* April 11, 1984, p. 29.

PART III

Anti-Satellite Weapons

1. Presidential Directive 37. Summarized in public document released by the White House, June 19, 1978.

2. U.S. Congress, Senate Committee on Foreign Relations, Subcommittee on Arms Control: Arms Control and the Militarization of Space: Hearings on Arms Control, 97th Congress, 2d session, September 20, 1982; testimony by Robert W. Buchheim.

3. Ibid., testimony by Eugene Rostow.

4. Ibid., testimony by Richard D. DeLauer. U.S. Congress, House Committee on Armed Services, Subcommittee on Research and Development, Hearings on Arms Control, March 17, 1983; testimony by Robert S. Cooper.

5. Nicholas L. Johnson, *The Soviet Year in Space: 1982.* Colorado Springs: Teledyne Brown Engineering, January 1983.

6. Nicholas L. Johnson, *The Soviet Year in Space: 1981.* Colorado Springs: Teledyne Brown Engineering, January 1982.

7. Nicholas L. Johnson, *The Soviet Year in Space: 1982,* op. cit.

8. Stephen M. Meyer, "Soviet Military Programs and the 'New High Ground.'" *Survival,* September–October, 1983.

9. U.S. Department of Defense. *Soviet Military Power—1983.* March 1983.

10. Stephen M. Meyer, "Soviet Military Programs and the 'New High Ground,'" op. cit.

11. Nicholas L. Johnson, *The Soviet Year in Space: 1982,* op. cit.

12. B. Jasani, ed. *Outer Space—A New Dimension of the Arms Race.* London: Stockholm International Peace Research Institute, Taylor & Francis, 1982.

13. Nicholas L. Johnson, *The Soviet Year in Space: 1982,* op. cit.

14. U.S. Congress, House Committee on Foreign Affairs and Senate Foreign Relations Committee. Fiscal Year 1984

Arms Control Impact Statements, 98th Congress, 1st session; submitted to the Congress by the President Pursuant to Section 36 of the Arms Control and Disarmament Act, April 1983; see especially pp. 131–34 and 265–67.

15. R. Jeffrey Smith, "The Search for a Nuclear Sanctuary," *Science,* Vol. 221 (July 1, 1983), p. 30.

16. The U.S. test of June 10, 1984, in which a dummy warhead was destroyed, produced debris spread over tens of kilometers. The photographic data obtained by a tracking telescope is reproduced in *Aviation Week & Space Technology,* June 18, 1984, p. 20.

17. R. Jeffrey Smith, *Science,* Vol. 224 (May 18, 1984), pp. 693–96.

18. *Science,* op. cit.

19. Ibid.

20. Ibid.

Treaty Between the United States of America and the Union of Soviet Socialist Republics on the Limitation of Anti-Ballistic Missile Systems

Signed at Moscow May 26, 1972

The United States of America and the Union of Soviet Socialist Republics, hereinafter referred to as the Parties,

Proceeding from the premise that nuclear war would have devastating consequences for all mankind,

Considering that effective measures to limit anti-ballistic missile systems would be a substantial factor in curbing the race in strategic offensive arms and would lead to a decrease in the risk of outbreak of war involving nuclear weapons,

Proceeding from the premise that the limitation of anti-ballistic missile systems, as well as certain agreed measures with respect to the limitation of strategic offensive arms, would contribute to the creation of more favorable conditions for further negotiations on limiting strategic arms,

Mindful of their obligations under Article VI of the Treaty on the Non-Proliferation of Nuclear Weapons,

Declaring their intention to achieve at the earliest possible date the cessation of the nuclear arms race and to take effective measures toward reductions in strategic arms, nuclear disarmament, and general and complete disarmament,

Desiring to contribute to the relaxation of international tension and the strengthening of trust between States,

Have agreed as follows:

Article I

1. Each party undertakes to limit anti-ballistic missile (ABM) systems and to adopt other measures in accordance with the provisions of this Treaty.

2. Each Party undertakes not to deploy ABM systems for a defense of the territory of its country and not to provide a base for such a defense, and not to deploy ABM systems for defense of an individual region except as provided for in Article III of this Treaty.

Article II

1. For the purpose of this Treaty an ABM system is a system to counter strategic ballistic missiles or their elements in flight trajectory, currently consisting of:

   (a) ABM interceptor missiles, which are interceptor missiles constructed and deployed for an ABM role, or of a type tested in an ABM mode;

   (b) ABM launchers, which are launchers constructed and deployed for launching ABM interceptor missiles; and

   (c) ABM radars, which are radars constructed and deployed for an ABM role, or of a type tested in an ABM mode.

2. The ABM system components listed in paragraph 1 of this Article include those which are:

   (a) operational;
   (b) under construction;
   (c) undergoing testing;
   (d) undergoing overhaul, repair or conversion; or
   (e) mothballed.

Article III

Each Party undertakes not to deploy ABM systems or their components except that:

(a) within one ABM system deployment area having a radius of one hundred and fifty kilometers and centered on the Party's national capital, a Party may deploy: (1) no more than one hundred ABM launchers and no more than one hundred ABM interceptor missiles at launch sites, and (2) ABM radars within no more than six ABM radar complexes, the area of each complex being circular and having a diameter of no more than three kilometers; and

(b) within one ABM system deployment area having a radius of one hundred and fifty kilometers and containing ICBM silo launchers, a Party may deploy: (1) no more than one hundred ABM launchers and no more than one hundred ABM interceptor missiles at launch sites, (2) two large phased-array ABM radars comparable in potential to corresponding ABM radars operational or under construction on the date of signature of the Treaty in an ABM system deployment area containing ICBM silo launchers, and (3) no more than eighteen ABM radars each having a potential less than the potential of the smaller of the above-mentioned two large phased-array ABM radars.

Article IV

The limitations provided for in Article III shall not apply to ABM systems or their components used for development or testing, and located within current or additionally agreed test ranges. Each Party may have no more than a total of fifteen ABM launchers at test ranges.

Article V

1. Each Party undertakes not to develop, test, or deploy ABM systems or components which are sea-based, air-based, space-based, or mobile land-based.

2. Each Party undertakes not to develop, test, or deploy

ABM launchers for launching more than one ABM interceptor missile at a time from each launcher, nor to modify deployed launchers to provide them with such a capability, nor
to develop, test, or deploy automatic or semi-automatic or
other similar systems for rapid reload of ABM launchers.

Article VI

To enhance assurance of the effectiveness of the limitations
on ABM systems and their components provided by this
Treaty, each Party undertakes:

(a) not to give missiles, launchers, or radars, other than
ABM interceptor missiles, ABM launchers, or ABM radars, capabilities to counter strategic ballistic missiles or
their elements in flight trajectory, and not to test them in
an ABM mode; and

(b) not to deploy in the future radars for early warning
of strategic ballistic missile attack except at locations along
the periphery of its national territory and oriented outward.

Article VII

Subject to the provisions of this Treaty, modernization and
replacement of ABM systems or their components may be
carried out.

Article VIII

ABM systems or their components in excess of the numbers or outside the areas specified in this Treaty, as well as
ABM systems or their components prohibited by this Treaty,
shall be destroyed or dismantled under agreed procedures
within the shortest possible agreed period of time.

Article IX

To assure the viability and effectiveness of this Treaty, each
Party undertakes not to transfer to other States, and not to

deploy outside its national territory, ABM systems or their components limited by this Treaty.

Article X

Each Party undertakes not to assume any international obligations which would conflict with this Treaty.

Article XI

The Parties undertake to continue active negotiations for limitations on strategic offensive arms.

Article XII

1. For the purpose of providing assurance of compliance with the provisions of this Treaty, each Party shall use national technical means of verification at its disposal in a manner consistent with generally recognized principles of international law.

2. Each Party undertakes not to interfere with the national technical means of verification of the other Party operating in accordance with paragraph 1 of this Article.

3. Each Party undertakes not to use deliberate concealment measures which impede verification by national technical means of compliance with the provisions of this Treaty. This obligation shall not require changes in current construction, assembly, conversion, or overhaul practices.

Article XIII

1. To promote the objectives and implementation of the provisions of this Treaty, the Parties shall establish promptly a Standing Consultative Commission, within the framework of which they will:

(a) consider questions concerning compliance with the obligations assumed and related situations which may be considered ambiguous;

(b) provide on a voluntary basis such information as

either Party considers necessary to assure confidence in compliance with the obligations assumed;

(c) consider questions involving unintended interference with national technical means of verification;

(d) consider possible changes in the strategic situation which have a bearing on the provisions of this Treaty;

(e) agree upon procedures and dates for destruction or dismantling of ABM systems or their components in cases provided for by the provisions of this Treaty;

(f) consider, as appropriate, possible proposals for further increasing the viability of this Treaty, including proposals for amendments in accordance with the provisions of this Treaty;

(g) consider, as appropriate, proposals for further measures aimed at limiting strategic arms.

2. The Parties through consultation shall establish, and may amend as appropriate, Regulations for the Standing Consultative Commission governing procedures, composition and other relevant matters.

Article XIV

1. Each Party may propose amendments to this Treaty. Agreed amendments shall enter into force in accordance with the procedures governing the entry into force of this Treaty.

2. Five years after entry into force of this Treaty, and at five-year intervals thereafter, the Parties shall together conduct a review of this Treaty.

Article XV

1. This Treaty shall be of unlimited duration.

2. Each Party shall, in exercising its national sovereignty, have the right to withdraw from this Treaty if it decides that extraordinary events related to the subject matter of this Treaty have jeopardized its supreme interests. It shall give notice of its decision to the other Party six months prior to withdrawal from the Treaty. Such notice shall include a state-

ment of the extraordinary events the notifying Party regards as having jeopardized its supreme interests.

Article XVI

1. This Treaty shall be subject to ratification in accordance with the constitutional procedures of each Party. The Treaty shall enter into force on the day of the exchange of instruments of ratification.

2. This Treaty shall be registered pursuant to Article 102 of the Charter of the United Nations.

DONE at Moscow on May 26, 1972, in two copies, each in the English and Russian languages, both texts being equally authentic.

FOR THE UNITED STATES OF AMERICA	FOR THE UNION OF SOVIET SOCIALIST REPUBLICS
|s| RICHARD NIXON	|s| L. I. BREZHNEV
President of the United States of America	General Secretary of the Central Committee of the CPSU

Protocol to the Treaty Between the United States of America and the Union of Soviet Socialist Republics on the Limitation of Anti-Ballistic Missile Systems

Signed at Moscow July 3, 1974
Entered into force May 24, 1976

The United States of America and the Union of Soviet Socialist Republics, hereinafter referred to as the Parties,
Proceeding from the Basic Principles of Relations between

the United States of America and the Union of Soviet Socialist Republics signed on May 29, 1972,

Desiring to further the objectives of the Treaty between the United States of America and the Union of Soviet Socialist Republics on the Limitation of Anti-Ballistic Missile Systems signed on May 26, 1972, hereinafter referred to as the Treaty,

Reaffirming their conviction that the adoption of further measures for the limitation of strategic arms would contribute to strengthening international peace and security,

Proceeding from the premise that further limitation of anti-ballistic missile systems will create more favorable conditions for the completion of work on a permanent agreement on more complete measures for the limitation of strategic offensive arms,

Have agreed as follows:

Article I

1. Each Party shall be limited at any one time to a single area out of the two provided in Article III of the Treaty for deployment of anti-ballistic missile (ABM) systems or their components and accordingly shall not exercise its right to deploy an ABM system or its components in the second of the two ABM system deployment areas permitted by Article III of the Treaty, except as an exchange of one permitted area for the other in accordance with Article II of this Protocol.

2. Accordingly, except as permitted by Article II of this Protocol: the United States of America shall not deploy an ABM system or its components in the area centered on its capital, as permitted by Article III(a) of the Treaty, and the Soviet Union shall not deploy an ABM system or its components in the deployment area of intercontinental ballistic missile (ICBM) silo launchers permitted by Article III(b) of the Treaty.

Article II

1. Each Party shall have the right to dismantle or destroy its ABM system and the components thereof in the area

where they are presently deployed and to deploy an ABM system or its components in the alternative area permitted by Article III of the Treaty, provided that prior to initiation of construction, notification is given in accord with the procedure agreed to by the Standing Consultative Commission, during the year beginning October 3, 1977, and ending October 2, 1978, or during any year which commences at five year intervals thereafter, those being the years for periodic review of the Treaty, as provided in Article XIV of the Treaty. This right may be exercised only once.

2. Accordingly, in the event of such notice, the United States would have the right to dismantle or destroy the ABM system and its components in the deployment area of ICBM silo launchers and to deploy an ABM system or its components in an area centered on its capital, as permitted by Article III(a) of the Treaty, and the Soviet Union would have the right to dismantle or destroy the ABM system and its components in the area centered on its capital and to deploy an ABM system or its components in an area containing ICBM silo launchers, as permitted by Article III(b) of the Treaty.

3. Dismantling or destruction and deployment of ABM systems or their components and the notification thereof shall be carried out in accordance with Article VIII of the ABM Treaty and procedures agreed to in the Standing Consultative Commission.

Article III

The rights and obligations established by the Treaty remain in force and shall be complied with by the Parties except to the extent modified by this Protocol. In particular, the deployment of an ABM system or its components within the area selected shall remain limited by the levels and other requirements established by the Treaty.

Article IV

This Protocol shall be subject to ratification in accordance with the constitutional procedures of each Party. It shall enter into force on the day of the exchange of instruments of ratification and shall thereafter be considered an integral part of the Treaty.

Done at Moscow on July 3, 1974, in duplicate, in the English and Russian languages, both texts being equally authentic.

For the United States of America:

RICHARD NIXON

President of the United States of America

For the Union of Soviet Socialist Republics:

L. I. BREZHNEV

General Secretary of the Central Committee of the CPSU

A Treaty Limiting Anti-Satellite Weapons

Preamble

Article I

Each Party undertakes not to destroy, damage, render inoperable, or change the flight trajectory of space objects of other States.

Article II

1. Each Party undertakes not to place in orbit around the earth weapons for destroying, damaging, rendering inoperable, or changing the flight trajectory of space objects, or for damaging objects in the atmosphere or on the ground.

2. Each Party undertakes not to install such weapons on celestial bodies, or station such weapons in outer space in any other manner.

3. Each Party undertakes not to test such weapons in space or against space objects.

Article III

1. For the purpose of providing assurance of compliance with the provisions of this treaty, each Party shall use national technical means of verification at its disposal in a manner consistent with generally recognized principles of international law.

2. Verification by national technical means shall be supplemented, as appropriate, by such cooperative measures for contributing to the effectiveness of verification by national technical means as the Parties shall agree upon in the Standing Consultative Commission.

3. Each Party undertakes not to interfere with the national technical means of verification of the other Party operating in accordance with paragraph 1 of this Article.

4. Each Party undertakes not to use deliberate concealment measures which impede verification by national technical means of compliance with this treaty.

Article IV

1. To promote the objectives and implementation of the provisions of this treaty, the Parties shall use the Standing Consultative Commission, established by the Memorandum of Understanding Between the Government of the United States of America and the Government of the Union of Soviet Socialist Republics regarding the Establishment of a Standing Consultative Commission of December 21, 1972.

2. Within the framework of the Standing Consultative Commission, with respect to this treaty, the Parties will:

a) consider questions concerning compliance with the obligations assumed and related situations which may be considered ambiguous;

b) provide on a voluntary basis such information as either Party considers necessary to assure confidence in compliance with the obligations assumed;

c) consider questions involving unintended interference with national technical means of verification, and questions involving unintended impeding of verification by national technical means of compliance with the provisions of this treaty;

d) consider, as appropriate, cooperative measures contributing to the effectiveness of verification by national technical means;

e) consider possible changes in the strategic situation which have a bearing on the provisions of this treaty, including the activities of other States;

f) consider, as appropriate, possible proposals for further increasing the viability of this treaty, including proposals for amendments in accordance with the provisions of this treaty.

Article V

The Parties undertake to begin, promptly after the entry into force of this treaty, active negotiations with the objective of achieving, as soon as possible, agreement on further measures for the limitation and reduction of weapons subject to limitation in Article II of this treaty.

Article VI

In order to ensure the viability and effectiveness of this treaty, each Party undertakes not to circumvent the provisions of this treaty, through any other State or States, in any other manner.

Article VII

Each party undertakes not to assume any international obligation which would conflict with this treaty.

Article VIII

1. Each Party may propose amendments to this treaty.

2. Agreed amendments shall enter into force in accordance with the procedures governing the entry into force of this treaty.

Article IX

This treaty shall be of unlimited duration.

Article X

Each Party shall, in exercising its national sovereignty, have the right to withdraw from this treaty if it decides that extraordinary events related to the subject matter of this treaty have jeopardized its supreme interests. It shall give notice of its decisions to the other Party six months prior to withdrawal from the treaty. Such notice shall include a statement of the extraordinary events the notifying Party regards as having jeopardized its supreme interests.

Article XI

1. This treaty shall be subject to ratification in accordance with the constitutional procedures of each Party.

2. This treaty shall enter into force on the day of the exchange of instruments of ratification.

Article XII

1. Done in two copies, each in the English and Russian languages, both texts being equally authentic.

2. This treaty shall be registered pursuant to Article '0? of the Charter of the United Nations.

Answers to Questions Posed by Senate Foreign Relations Committee to Richard Garwin, Noel Gayler, and Kurt Gottfried on May 18, 1983

June 3, 1983

QUESTION 1: What do you regard as the most destabilizing developments in current and future space programs?

RESPONSE: In our view the most destabilizing aspects of current and future U.S. and Soviet space programs are:

a) The continuing testing of the Soviet ASAT;

b) the upcoming tests of the U.S. F-15 ASAT;

c) the absence of any negotiations to limit the further growth of ASAT capabilities; and

d) President Reagan's speech of March 23, 1983, setting a U.S. course towards a perfect defense against all nuclear-armed missiles (as interpreted on national television by Secretary of Defense Weinberger on March 27, 1983).

Taken together, these actions and policies are:

i) planting the seeds for a capacity that will, if allowed to grow, threaten our space-borne warning systems with preemptive attack; and

ii) seriously imperil the ABM treaty, and with it our confidence that our retaliatory forces continue to retain the ability to penetrate Soviet defenses.

Even though there is no scientific justification for holding out hope for a leakproof space-based defense against nuclear weapons, the quest for such a defense will, even if futile, have destabilizing consequences. In particular, the prospect of a space-based BMD system is certain to spawn the development of space mines by the adversary, which will hound the BMD platforms to assure penetration of ICBMs. Space mines will be developed even if, as is most probable, no BMD capability is ever achieved, and these mines will then threaten all objects in space, whether they carry weapons or not. This could lead to war in space as a prelude to war on earth.

QUESTION 2: In his March 23 speech, President Reagan stated that if laser defense was "paired with offensive systems, they can be viewed as fostering an aggressive policy."

a) Do you agree with this assessment?

b) If so, why? If not, why not?

c) Some have argued that if we can reduce offensive weapons to the point that they no longer appear offensive then there would be no need for a space-based BMD system. Do you agree?

RESPONSE:

a) We agree that an effective defense against nuclear weapons, when paired with the existence of offensive systems, would "support an aggressive policy." But as we make clear in our responses to Questions 9 and 10, we do not accept the underlying assumption in the president's statement, to wit, that an effective defense against missile-borne nuclear warheads can be built.

b) It can support coercive policy. In fact, held by one side, such capabilities would allow world domination. Paradoxically, if offensive and perfect defensive weapons were available to both sides (leaving aside the rest of the world for the moment), there would be no feeling of serenity, since it would be quite obvious that the effectiveness of a defense might be destroyed catastrophically by sabotage, deception, or the like

c) We doubt that either the Soviet Union or the United States is likely to give up offensive weapons and the insurance of deterrence by threat of retaliation. Yes, we suspect that it would be easier to negotiate away offensive weapons than to build an effective space-based BMD system.

QUESTION 3: Some government officials contend that any Soviet missile can serve as an ASAT launcher. Accordingly, it is argued, verification of an ASAT ban could be difficult, if not impossible. Do you agree with this view?

RESPONSE: In all twenty reported tests of their ASAT interceptor over the past fifteen years, the Soviets have used only one launch booster, a missile based on the old SS-9 "heavy" ICBM. Therefore, the Soviets lack ASAT experience with any other missile. Anyone who imagines that "any Soviet missile can serve as an ASAT launcher" displays a lack of awareness of the difficulties that habitually plague space hardware programs, and the Soviet ASAT program in particular. If the Soviets sought to use a different booster, they would confront several obstacles. First, if the interceptor itself has been specially designed to fit onto the SS-9 missile, it would have to be redesigned to fit a new booster, and the new configuration would require space tests to confirm that the entire system worked properly in its new form. Such tests would be visible to U.S. surveillance systems. Second, the bulk of Soviet space launch boosters and operational ICBMs have launch- and payload-weights no greater than the SS-9, and the Soviets would gain little by putting their ASAT on a different missile that was only comparable or inferior to the current booster. Third, the SS-9 itself has been phased out and replaced by the SS-18. If the Soviets sought to put their ASAT interceptor on a silo-based SS-18, then the silo too must be designed to accommodate the extra length and special launch-preparation requirements of the interceptor. Major modifications to operational silos, if they were required, would be monitored by U.S. intelligence systems, as could space test of the new SS-18/ASAT configuration.

Finally, there are Soviet boosters that are larger than the SS-9, such as those used for the Soyuz and Salyut programs, and these in principle could carry the Soviet ASAT to higher altitudes. However, attacking satellites at higher altitudes places greater demands upon an interceptor—e.g., greater homing range, greater guidance accuracy, greater maneuvering power. Such improvements in an interceptor would also require space tests to confirm. So even if the Soviet interceptor could be mounted on a different booster, that alone could not increase the threat it poses, as long as further space tests are banned.

A prompt ban on further ASAT space tests would serve U.S. interests by inhibiting any such improvements to the current Soviet ASAT system.

QUESTION 4: The Soviets have tabled a draft treaty that would ban all weapons from space. This treaty would apparently allow the Soviet Union to retain its current ASAT. How does your proposal differ with the Soviet proposal? Do you see the Soviet draft treaty as a realistic basis for negotiations?

RESPONSE: The Soviet Draft Treaty placed before the UN in 1981 suggests a serious interest in reaching an arms control agreement in space weaponry. The Soviet draft contains some elements that are worthy of serious consideration, even though the treaty draft is not acceptable as it stands. The degree to which it is unacceptable can be gauged from the remainder of this response.

The most important differences between the Soviet draft and the one put forward by us are that our draft forbids:

a) Tests against space objects in one's possession;

b) Tests from weapons on the ground;

c) Tests against objects on the ground or in the atmosphere from weapons in space.

Furthermore, our draft does not permit attacks against space objects that are in violation of the treaty's provisions; it addresses this problem in the traditional manner, by providing for withdrawal from the obligations of the treaty after due notice. Finally, our draft is bilateral.

QUESTION 5: Your proposal bans ASAT testing but not ground-based ASAT deployments. Given the fact that the Soviets have tested their ASAT, would your proposal be in effect a one-sided ban directed against the United States? If your proposal were in force, what incentives would the Soviet Union have for agreeing to dismantle their ASAT?

RESPONSE: Our discussion shows that our proposed treaty would not be to the "one-sided" disadvantage of the United States. If our treaty were to come into force, the USSR will have a tested ASAT, but one which has shown itself to be very unreliable, while the U.S. would have under advanced development a more flexible and potent ASAT that had not yet been tested. Under the treaty regime we propose, the U.S. would probably be closer to a prompt, flexible, all-altitude ASAT system than the USSR, while neither existing capability would pose much of a threat to those satellites on either side that are vital if nuclear war should break out.

In striking a balance of advantage versus disadvantage, one must consider factors other than the capabilities of the two ASAT systems. Since the United States is, on balance, more dependent on satellites for its security, anything that inhibits the evolution of the Soviet ASAT threat could be viewed as a "one-sided" advantage for the U.S.

The main incentive the Soviets would have for agreeing to dismantle their ASAT would be their awareness that their current ASAT system would become progressively obsolete anyway. In the absence of space tests, the Soviets would be left with an unreliable interceptor based upon 1960s technology, while the U.S. remained free to adopt sophisticated measures for protecting and diversifying its satellite functions.

QUESTION 6: Even if the Soviet ASAT capability is viewed as limited, does it not amount to a significant threat, given the high level of U.S. dependence upon a relatively small number of satellites?

RESPONSE: The Soviet ASAT, as presently constituted, could, over a period of several days, destroy a significant portion of our space-based capability for photo reconnaissance, which is of greatest importance in peacetime. It has quite limited capability against the remainder of our space-based command, control, communications, and intelligence systems; in particular, it has virtually no capability against that portion of the system that would be employed by the strategic forces in wartime. Nevertheless, the U.S. should consider the desirability of various measures for protecting its satellites, or, for example, of providing ground-based back-up C systems for satellites important to theater conflicts.

QUESTION 7: We have previously used national technical means of verification to observe the dismantling of launchers.

a) Did you consider an ASAT ban involving the dismantling of Soviet ASAT launchers?

b) If yes, why did you not adopt this as your proposal?

RESPONSE: a) We have considered an ASAT ban involving the dismantling of Soviet ASAT launchers.

b) We did not adopt this as our proposal because we see no way in which the Soviets could verify that the United States had destroyed its F-15 ASAT system, and the difficulty of negotiating a nonsymmetric treaty far exceeds the additional benefit we would obtain by destruction of the existing Soviet ASAT. Furthermore, dismantling of the known Soviet launch sites would not guarantee that the Soviet Union did not retain some ASAT capability.

Our draft treaty does include a provision (Article V) requiring the sides to begin negotiations on this issue immediately after a ban on space tests of ASATs is reached. However, we also recognized that provisions for dismantling ASAT systems could be quite complicated, and would, at best, require long negotiations. Hence we view our proposed ban on further ASAT space tests as an urgent and indispensable first step toward any wider ASAT arms control measures. (For other closely related remarks, see our response to Question 12).

QUESTION 8: Senator Matsunaga and I [Senator Pell] are cosponsoring a concurrent resolution, S. Con. Res. 16, expressing the sense of the Congress that the President should initiate talks with the Soviet Union and other governments to explore opportunities for cooperative East-West ventures in space, as an alternative to an arms race. Do you support such a resolution?

RESPONSE: We support the Resolution sponsored by Senators Matsunaga and Pell. We agree that cooperation in space would be an important ingredient in creating an atmosphere that would inhibit confrontation. But we do not think that such cooperation, by itself, would preclude an arms race in space. Cooperation should be viewed as one component in a diplomacy that seeks to avert such a race; the other, indispensable component is a treaty that restricts the evolution of space-based weapons.

QUESTION 9: Do you believe that a space-based ABM system of even limited capacity could ever be built?

RESPONSE: A spaced-based ABM system of *very* limited capacity could be built *provided* the enemy abstained from taking rather simple and relatively cheap countermeasures.

QUESTION 10: Do you believe that such a system could ever effectively protect the United States from nuclear attacks?

RESPONSE: We are persuaded that such a system could never effectively protect the United States from an intentional large-scale missile attack from the Soviet Union, and even less could it protect against the systems the Soviets would develop in order to penetrate, circumvent, and destroy such a defensive system.

QUESTION 11: If we do not institute effective controls on weapons in space, what do you think will be the result?

RESPONSE: Without an effective ban on weapons in space, and a ban on anti-satellite tests and activities, we are persuaded that the striving for ASAT and ABM capabilities could lead to war in space during what would otherwise have been peacetime, which would almost certainly lead to war on earth. This is so because it is very much simpler to achieve an ASAT capability than an ABM capability. Satellites are intrinsically more vulnerable than ballistic missiles; furthermore, the nature of the satellite's trajectory allows ample time for target acquisition, and for repeated attacks. Any space-based BMD capability, therefore, has an inherent ASAT capability, even if its potency against ICBMs is actually minimal. In particular, such a nascent ABM system can preemptively destroy an imagined ABM system belonging to the other side. Furthermore, either side can, at an early stage, station space mines that have the capacity for preemptive destruction of any satellites carrying ABM systems deployed by the other.

QUESTION 12: Why doesn't your draft treaty ban land-based ASATs? Would you favor such a ban if effective verification could be worked out?

RESPONSE: Our treaty bans all *tests* of land-based ASATs in space or against objects in space. Effective verification of a provision that also bans *possession* of land-based ASATs would require very intrusive verification measures, including extensive on-site inspection. For example, the U.S. ASAT interceptor and its launch booster are fairly small and could readily be hidden in many places at U.S. military facilities. Even the U.S. might find such intrusive on-site inspection at military bases unacceptable. As for the Soviet ASAT, even though it is large it could be launched by some of the boosters used in the Soviet space program (see response to Question 3, however). Therefore dismantling of the launchers that have been used for Soviet ASAT test shots would not by itself guarantee that there was no remnant Soviet ASAT capability.

One must bear in mind that the existing Soviet ASAT is intrinsically of rather limited capability. The prevention of any significant enhancement of that capability should therefore be the *primary* objective of U.S. policy, not the elimination of a relatively minor threat.

We recognize that a comprehensive ban on ASAT possession would be desirable, and for that reason our draft treaty, through Article V, obligates the parties to promptly begin negotiations towards that end as soon as the ASAT test ban is in place. If a treaty that would adequately verify lack of possession could be formulated, we certainly would support it. But given the limited political capital and human resources available for any negotiation, and the urgent need for a viable restriction on the growth of ASAT capabilities, we do not favor a negotiation position that may sacrifice the attainment of an ASAT test ban to the search for a ban on possession.

Union of Concerned Scientists is an independent, non-profit organization of scientists and citizens concerned about the impact of advanced technology on society. Founded in 1969 in Cambridge, Massachusetts, UCS's research, public advocacy, and educational activities focus on nuclear arms control, energy policy, and nuclear-power safety.